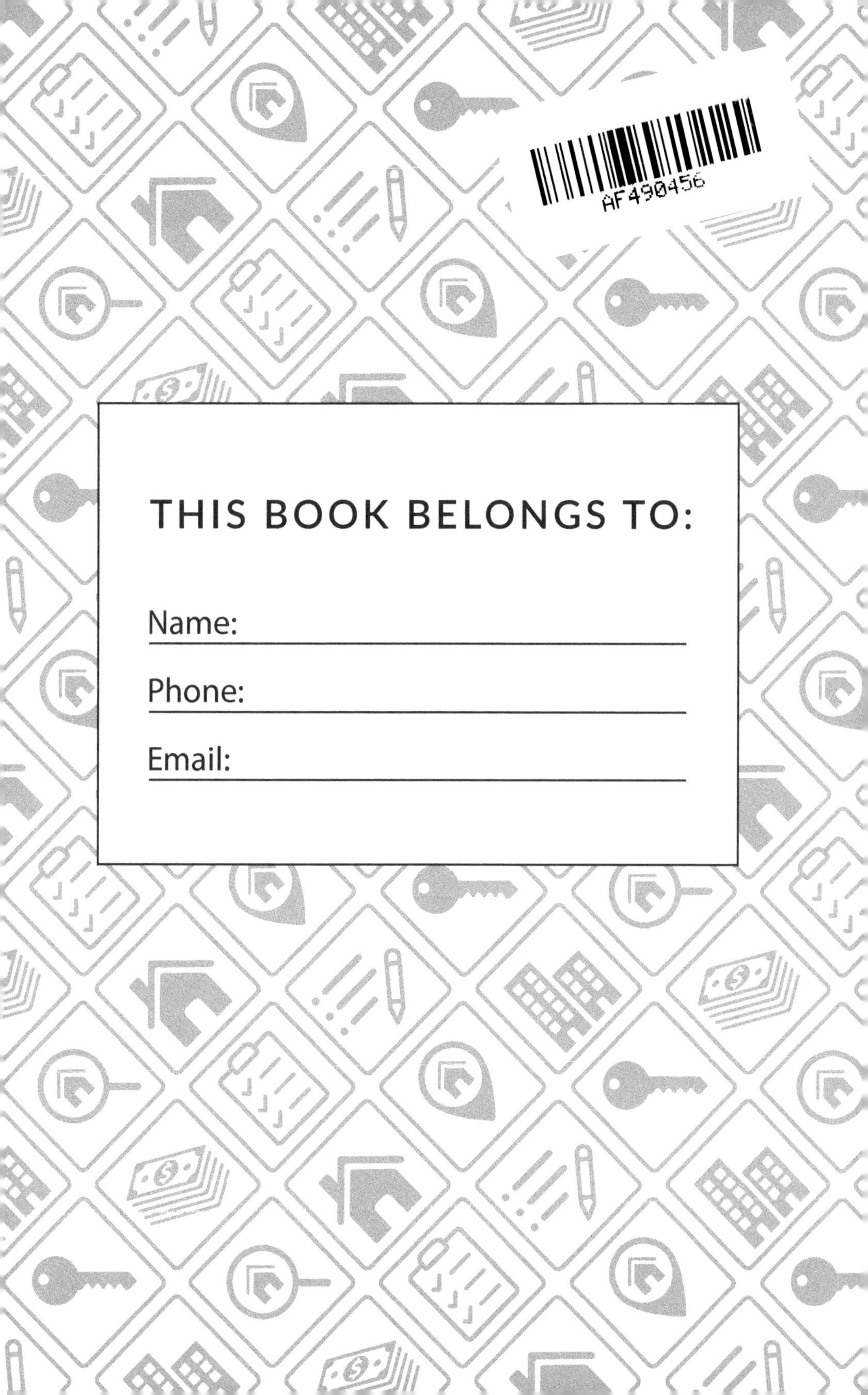


# THIS BOOK BELONGS TO:

Name:

Phone:

Email:

# IMPORTANT CONTACTS

| NAME | JOB | PHONE |
|---|---|---|
|  |  |  |
|  |  |  |
|  |  |  |
|  |  |  |
|  |  |  |
|  |  |  |
|  |  |  |
|  |  |  |
|  |  |  |
|  |  |  |
|  |  |  |
|  |  |  |
|  |  |  |
|  |  |  |
|  |  |  |
|  |  |  |
|  |  |  |
|  |  |  |
|  |  |  |
|  |  |  |
|  |  |  |
|  |  |  |

# IMPORTANT DATES

| DATE | NOTES AND REMINDERS |
| --- | --- |
|  |  |
|  |  |
|  |  |
|  |  |
|  |  |
|  |  |
|  |  |
|  |  |
|  |  |
|  |  |
|  |  |
|  |  |
|  |  |
|  |  |
|  |  |
|  |  |
|  |  |
|  |  |
|  |  |
|  |  |
|  |  |
|  |  |
|  |  |

# 1

# PROPERTY INFORMATION

| ADDRESS | |
|---|---|
| BEDROOMS | | BATHROOMS | | Sq. Ft. | |
| LOT SIZE | | YEAR BUILT | | SCHOOL DISTRICT | |
| ANNUAL TAX | | PRICE | |

# REALTOR INFORMATION

| NAME | |
|---|---|
| AGENCY | |
| PHONE | |
| EMAIL | |

## NOTES AND REMINDERS

# INSPECTION CHECKLIST

## INTERIOR

### FLOORING, WINDOWS & CEILING

**FLOOR**

☐ Age?

☐ Condition? _____________

**WINDOWS**

☐ Condition? _____________

**CEILING**

☐ Condition? _____________

### ROOMS

Y N

☐☐ Natural Lighting?

☐☐ Even Floors?

☐☐ Smoke Detectors?

☐☐ Carbon Monoxide Detector?

### WALLS

Y N

☐☐ Stains?

☐☐ Need Re-painting?

☐☐ Soundproof?

### STAIRS

Y N

☐☐ Creaky?

☐☐ Signs of Damage?

### DOORS

Y N

☐☐ Open & Close Property

☐☐ Weather Proofed

☐☐ Working Doorbell

### BATHROOM

Y N

☐☐ Stain-free?

☐☐ Mildew/Mold-free?

☐☐ Leak-free?

☐☐ Cabinet & Storage Space?

☐☐ Working Fans?

☐☐ Functioning Toilet?

### KITCHEN

Y N

☐☐ Stain-free?

☐☐ Mildew/Mold-free?

☐☐ Leak-free?

☐☐ Cabinet & Storage Space?

☐☐ Working Fans?

☐☐ Working Garbage Disposal?

## EXTERIOR

### UP-TO-DATE SYSTEMS

☐ Hire Home Inspector [*before purchase*]

☐ Electrical

☐ A/C

☐ Heating

☐ Security

☐ Plumbing

☐ Water

☐ Sewer Insulation

### ROOF

Y N

☐☐ Sagging Roof Line?

☐☐ Discoloration?

☐☐ Holes?

### FOUNDATION, DRIVEWAY, & POOL

**FOUNDATION**

☐ Visible Cracks? _____________

**DRIVEWAY**

☐ Visible Cracks? _____________

**POOL**

☐ Visible Cracks? _____________

☐ Above Ground? _____________

### GARAGE

Y N

☐☐ Functional - Manual?

☐☐ Functional - Remote?

☐ N/A

### SIDING

Y N

☐☐ Paint Peeling?

☐☐ Cracks/Splits?

### LANDSCAPING & CURB APPEAL

☐ Trees - Condition?

_____________

☐ Lawn [*front*] - Condition?

_____________

☐ Lawn [*back*] - Condition?

_____________

☐ Fences - Condition?

_____________

☐ Landscaping - Condition?

_____________

2

# PROPERTY INFORMATION

| ADDRESS | | | | | |
|---|---|---|---|---|---|
| BEDROOMS | | BATHROOMS | | Sq. Ft. | |
| LOT SIZE | | YEAR BUILT | | SCHOOL DISTRICT | |
| ANNUAL TAX | | PRICE | | | |

# REALTOR INFORMATION

| NAME | |
|---|---|
| AGENCY | |
| PHONE | |
| EMAIL | |

## NOTES AND REMINDERS

# INSPECTION CHECKLIST

## INTERIOR

### FLOORING, WINDOWS & CEILING

**FLOOR**
- ☐ Age?
- ☐ Condition? ____________

**WINDOWS**
- ☐ Condition? ____________

**CEILING**
- ☐ Condition? ____________

### ROOMS

Y N
- ☐☐ Natural Lighting?
- ☐☐ Even Floors?
- ☐☐ Smoke Detectors?
- ☐☐ Carbon Monoxide Detector?

### WALLS

Y N
- ☐☐ Stains?
- ☐☐ Need Re-painting?
- ☐☐ Soundproof?

### STAIRS

Y N
- ☐☐ Creaky?
- ☐☐ Signs of Damage?

### DOORS

Y N
- ☐☐ Open & Close Property
- ☐☐ Weather Proofed
- ☐☐ Working Doorbell

### BATHROOM

Y N
- ☐☐ Stain-free?
- ☐☐ Mildew/Mold-free?
- ☐☐ Leak-free?
- ☐☐ Cabinet & Storage Space?
- ☐☐ Working Fans?
- ☐☐ Functioning Toilet?

### KITCHEN

Y N
- ☐☐ Stain-free?
- ☐☐ Mildew/Mold-free?
- ☐☐ Leak-free?
- ☐☐ Cabinet & Storage Space?
- ☐☐ Working Fans?
- ☐☐ Working Garbage Disposal?

## EXTERIOR

### UP-TO-DATE SYSTEMS

- ☐ Hire Home Inspector [*before purchase*]
- ☐ Electrical
- ☐ A/C
- ☐ Heating
- ☐ Security
- ☐ Plumbing
- ☐ Water
- ☐ Sewer Insulation

### ROOF

Y N
- ☐☐ Sagging Roof Line?
- ☐☐ Discoloration?
- ☐☐ Holes?

### FOUNDATION, DRIVEWAY, & POOL

**FOUNDATION**
- ☐ Visible Cracks? __________

**DRIVEWAY**
- ☐ Visible Cracks? __________

**POOL**
- ☐ Visible Cracks? __________
- ☐ Above Ground? __________

### GARAGE

Y N
- ☐☐ Functional - Manual?
- ☐☐ Functional - Remote?
- ☐ N/A

### SIDING

Y N
- ☐☐ Paint Peeling?
- ☐☐ Cracks/Splits?

### LANDSCAPING & CURB APPEAL

- ☐ Trees - Condition?
  ____________________

- ☐ Lawn [*front*] - Condition?
  ____________________

- ☐ Lawn [*back*] - Condition?
  ____________________

- ☐ Fences - Condition?
  ____________________

- ☐ Landscaping - Condition?
  ____________________

3

# PROPERTY INFORMATION

| ADDRESS | |
|---|---|
| BEDROOMS | | BATHROOMS | | Sq. Ft. | |
| LOT SIZE | | YEAR BUILT | | SCHOOL DISTRICT | |
| ANNUAL TAX | | PRICE | |

# REALTOR INFORMATION

| NAME | |
|---|---|
| AGENCY | |
| PHONE | |
| EMAIL | |

## NOTES AND REMINDERS

# INSPECTION CHECKLIST

## INTERIOR

### FLOORING, WINDOWS & CEILING

**FLOOR**
- ☐ Age?
- ☐ Condition? _____________

**WINDOWS**
- ☐ Condition? _____________

**CEILING**
- ☐ Condition? _____________

### ROOMS

Y N
- ☐☐ Natural Lighting?
- ☐☐ Even Floors?
- ☐☐ Smoke Detectors?
- ☐☐ Carbon Monoxide Detector?

### WALLS

Y N
- ☐☐ Stains?
- ☐☐ Need Re-painting?
- ☐☐ Soundproof?

### STAIRS

Y N
- ☐☐ Creaky?
- ☐☐ Signs of Damage?

### DOORS

Y N
- ☐☐ Open & Close Property
- ☐☐ Weather Proofed
- ☐☐ Working Doorbell

### BATHROOM

Y N
- ☐☐ Stain-free?
- ☐☐ Mildew/Mold-free?
- ☐☐ Leak-free?
- ☐☐ Cabinet & Storage Space?
- ☐☐ Working Fans?
- ☐☐ Functioning Toilet?

### KITCHEN

Y N
- ☐☐ Stain-free?
- ☐☐ Mildew/Mold-free?
- ☐☐ Leak-free?
- ☐☐ Cabinet & Storage Space?
- ☐☐ Working Fans?
- ☐☐ Working Garbage Disposal?

## EXTERIOR

### UP-TO-DATE SYSTEMS

- ☐ Hire Home Inspector [*before purchase*]
- ☐ Electrical
- ☐ A/C
- ☐ Heating
- ☐ Security
- ☐ Plumbing
- ☐ Water
- ☐ Sewer Insulation

### ROOF

Y N
- ☐☐ Sagging Roof Line?
- ☐☐ Discoloration?
- ☐☐ Holes?

### FOUNDATION, DRIVEWAY, & POOL

**FOUNDATION**
- ☐ Visible Cracks? _____________

**DRIVEWAY**
- ☐ Visible Cracks? _____________

**POOL**
- ☐ Visible Cracks? _____________
- ☐ Above Ground? _____________

### GARAGE

Y N
- ☐☐ Functional - Manual?
- ☐☐ Functional - Remote?
- ☐ N/A

### SIDING

Y N
- ☐☐ Paint Peeling?
- ☐☐ Cracks/Splits?

### LANDSCAPING & CURB APPEAL

- ☐ Trees - Condition?

_____________

- ☐ Lawn [*front*] - Condition?

_____________

- ☐ Lawn [*back*] - Condition?

_____________

- ☐ Fences - Condition?

_____________

- ☐ Landscaping - Condition?

_____________

4

# PROPERTY INFORMATION

| ADDRESS | |
|---|---|
| BEDROOMS | | BATHROOMS | | Sq. Ft. | |
| LOT SIZE | | YEAR BUILT | | SCHOOL DISTRICT | |
| ANNUAL TAX | | PRICE | |

# REALTOR INFORMATION

| NAME | |
|---|---|
| AGENCY | |
| PHONE | |
| EMAIL | |

## NOTES AND REMINDERS

# INSPECTION CHECKLIST

## INTERIOR

### FLOORING, WINDOWS & CEILING

**FLOOR**
- ☐ Age?
- ☐ Condition? ______________

**WINDOWS**
- ☐ Condition? ______________

**CEILING**
- ☐ Condition? ______________

### ROOMS

Y N
- ☐☐ Natural Lighting?
- ☐☐ Even Floors?
- ☐☐ Smoke Detectors?
- ☐☐ Carbon Monoxide Detector?

### WALLS

Y N
- ☐☐ Stains?
- ☐☐ Need Re-painting?
- ☐☐ Soundproof?

### STAIRS

Y N
- ☐☐ Creaky?
- ☐☐ Signs of Damage?

### DOORS

Y N
- ☐☐ Open & Close Property
- ☐☐ Weather Proofed
- ☐☐ Working Doorbell

### BATHROOM

Y N
- ☐☐ Stain-free?
- ☐☐ Mildew/Mold-free?
- ☐☐ Leak-free?
- ☐☐ Cabinet & Storage Space?
- ☐☐ Working Fans?
- ☐☐ Functioning Toilet?

### KITCHEN

Y N
- ☐☐ Stain-free?
- ☐☐ Mildew/Mold-free?
- ☐☐ Leak-free?
- ☐☐ Cabinet & Storage Space?
- ☐☐ Working Fans?
- ☐☐ Working Garbage Disposal?

## EXTERIOR

### UP-TO-DATE SYSTEMS

- ☐ Hire Home Inspector [*before purchase*]
- ☐ Electrical
- ☐ A/C
- ☐ Heating
- ☐ Security
- ☐ Plumbing
- ☐ Water
- ☐ Sewer Insulation

### ROOF

Y N
- ☐☐ Sagging Roof Line?
- ☐☐ Discoloration?
- ☐☐ Holes?

### FOUNDATION, DRIVEWAY, & POOL

**FOUNDATION**
- ☐ Visible Cracks? ___________

**DRIVEWAY**
- ☐ Visible Cracks? ___________

**POOL**
- ☐ Visible Cracks? ___________
- ☐ Above Ground? ___________

### GARAGE

Y N
- ☐☐ Functional - Manual?
- ☐☐ Functional - Remote?
- ☐ N/A

### SIDING

Y N
- ☐☐ Paint Peeling?
- ☐☐ Cracks/Splits?

### LANDSCAPING & CURB APPEAL

- ☐ Trees - Condition?

______________________

- ☐ Lawn [*front*] - Condition?

______________________

- ☐ Lawn [*back*] - Condition?

______________________

- ☐ Fences - Condition?

______________________

- ☐ Landscaping - Condition?

______________________

# 5

# PROPERTY INFORMATION

| ADDRESS | | | | | |
|---|---|---|---|---|---|
| BEDROOMS | | BATHROOMS | | Sq. Ft. | |
| LOT SIZE | | YEAR BUILT | | SCHOOL DISTRICT | |
| ANNUAL TAX | | PRICE | | | |

# REALTOR INFORMATION

| NAME | |
|---|---|
| AGENCY | |
| PHONE | |
| EMAIL | |

## NOTES AND REMINDERS

# INSPECTION CHECKLIST

## INTERIOR

### FLOORING, WINDOWS & CEILING

**FLOOR**

☐ Age?

☐ Condition? _____________

**WINDOWS**

☐ Condition? _____________

**CEILING**

☐ Condition? _____________

### ROOMS

Y N

☐☐ Natural Lighting?

☐☐ Even Floors?

☐☐ Smoke Detectors?

☐☐ Carbon Monoxide Detector?

### WALLS

Y N

☐☐ Stains?

☐☐ Need Re-painting?

☐☐ Soundproof?

### STAIRS

Y N

☐☐ Creaky?

☐☐ Signs of Damage?

### DOORS

Y N

☐☐ Open & Close Property

☐☐ Weather Proofed

☐☐ Working Doorbell

### BATHROOM

Y N

☐☐ Stain-free?

☐☐ Mildew/Mold-free?

☐☐ Leak-free?

☐☐ Cabinet & Storage Space?

☐☐ Working Fans?

☐☐ Functioning Toilet?

### KITCHEN

Y N

☐☐ Stain-free?

☐☐ Mildew/Mold-free?

☐☐ Leak-free?

☐☐ Cabinet & Storage Space?

☐☐ Working Fans?

☐☐ Working Garbage Disposal?

## EXTERIOR

### UP-TO-DATE SYSTEMS

☐ Hire Home Inspector [*before purchase*]

☐ Electrical

☐ A/C

☐ Heating

☐ Security

☐ Plumbing

☐ Water

☐ Sewer Insulation

### ROOF

Y N

☐☐ Sagging Roof Line?

☐☐ Discoloration?

☐☐ Holes?

### FOUNDATION, DRIVEWAY, & POOL

**FOUNDATION**

☐ Visible Cracks? _____________

**DRIVEWAY**

☐ Visible Cracks? _____________

**POOL**

☐ Visible Cracks? _____________

☐ Above Ground? _____________

### GARAGE

Y N

☐☐ Functional - Manual?

☐☐ Functional - Remote?

☐ N/A

### SIDING

Y N

☐☐ Paint Peeling?

☐☐ Cracks/Splits?

### LANDSCAPING & CURB APPEAL

☐ Trees - Condition?

_____________

☐ Lawn [*front*] - Condition?

_____________

☐ Lawn [*back*] - Condition?

_____________

☐ Fences - Condition?

_____________

☐ Landscaping - Condition?

_____________

# 6

# PROPERTY INFORMATION

| ADDRESS | | | | | |
|---|---|---|---|---|---|
| BEDROOMS | | BATHROOMS | | Sq. Ft. | |
| LOT SIZE | | YEAR BUILT | | SCHOOL DISTRICT | |
| ANNUAL TAX | | PRICE | | | |

# REALTOR INFORMATION

| NAME | |
|---|---|
| AGENCY | |
| PHONE | |
| EMAIL | |

## NOTES AND REMINDERS

# INSPECTION CHECKLIST

## INTERIOR

### FLOORING, WINDOWS & CEILING

**FLOOR**
- ☐ Age?
- ☐ Condition? _____________

**WINDOWS**
- ☐ Condition? _____________

**CEILING**
- ☐ Condition? _____________

### ROOMS

Y N
- ☐☐ Natural Lighting?
- ☐☐ Even Floors?
- ☐☐ Smoke Detectors?
- ☐☐ Carbon Monoxide Detector?

### WALLS

Y N
- ☐☐ Stains?
- ☐☐ Need Re-painting?
- ☐☐ Soundproof?

### STAIRS

Y N
- ☐☐ Creaky?
- ☐☐ Signs of Damage?

### DOORS

Y N
- ☐☐ Open & Close Property
- ☐☐ Weather Proofed
- ☐☐ Working Doorbell

### BATHROOM

Y N
- ☐☐ Stain-free?
- ☐☐ Mildew/Mold-free?
- ☐☐ Leak-free?
- ☐☐ Cabinet & Storage Space?
- ☐☐ Working Fans?
- ☐☐ Functioning Toilet?

### KITCHEN

Y N
- ☐☐ Stain-free?
- ☐☐ Mildew/Mold-free?
- ☐☐ Leak-free?
- ☐☐ Cabinet & Storage Space?
- ☐☐ Working Fans?
- ☐☐ Working Garbage Disposal?

## EXTERIOR

### UP-TO-DATE SYSTEMS

- ☐ Hire Home Inspector [*before purchase*]
- ☐ Electrical
- ☐ A/C
- ☐ Heating
- ☐ Security
- ☐ Plumbing
- ☐ Water
- ☐ Sewer Insulation

### ROOF

Y N
- ☐☐ Sagging Roof Line?
- ☐☐ Discoloration?
- ☐☐ Holes?

### FOUNDATION, DRIVEWAY, & POOL

**FOUNDATION**
- ☐ Visible Cracks? _____________

**DRIVEWAY**
- ☐ Visible Cracks? _____________

**POOL**
- ☐ Visible Cracks? _____________
- ☐ Above Ground? _____________

### GARAGE

Y N
- ☐☐ Functional - Manual?
- ☐☐ Functional - Remote?
- ☐ N/A

### SIDING

Y N
- ☐☐ Paint Peeling?
- ☐☐ Cracks/Splits?

### LANDSCAPING & CURB APPEAL

- ☐ Trees - Condition?

_____________________

- ☐ Lawn [*front*] - Condition?

_____________________

- ☐ Lawn [*back*] - Condition?

_____________________

- ☐ Fences - Condition?

_____________________

- ☐ Landscaping - Condition?

_____________________

**7**

# PROPERTY INFORMATION

| ADDRESS | | | | |
|---|---|---|---|---|
| BEDROOMS | | BATHROOMS | | Sq. Ft. |
| LOT SIZE | | YEAR BUILT | | SCHOOL DISTRICT |
| ANNUAL TAX | | PRICE | | |

# REALTOR INFORMATION

| NAME | |
|---|---|
| AGENCY | |
| PHONE | |
| EMAIL | |

## NOTES AND REMINDERS

# INSPECTION CHECKLIST

## INTERIOR

### FLOORING, WINDOWS & CEILING

**FLOOR**
- ☐ Age?
- ☐ Condition? _____________

**WINDOWS**
- ☐ Condition? _____________

**CEILING**
- ☐ Condition? _____________

### ROOMS

Y N
- ☐☐ Natural Lighting?
- ☐☐ Even Floors?
- ☐☐ Smoke Detectors?
- ☐☐ Carbon Monoxide Detector?

### WALLS

Y N
- ☐☐ Stains?
- ☐☐ Need Re-painting?
- ☐☐ Soundproof?

### STAIRS

Y N
- ☐☐ Creaky?
- ☐☐ Signs of Damage?

### DOORS

Y N
- ☐☐ Open & Close Property
- ☐☐ Weather Proofed
- ☐☐ Working Doorbell

### BATHROOM

Y N
- ☐☐ Stain-free?
- ☐☐ Mildew/Mold-free?
- ☐☐ Leak-free?
- ☐☐ Cabinet & Storage Space?
- ☐☐ Working Fans?
- ☐☐ Functioning Toilet?

### KITCHEN

Y N
- ☐☐ Stain-free?
- ☐☐ Mildew/Mold-free?
- ☐☐ Leak-free?
- ☐☐ Cabinet & Storage Space?
- ☐☐ Working Fans?
- ☐☐ Working Garbage Disposal?

## EXTERIOR

### UP-TO-DATE SYSTEMS

- ☐ Hire Home Inspector [*before purchase*]
- ☐ Electrical
- ☐ A/C
- ☐ Heating
- ☐ Security
- ☐ Plumbing
- ☐ Water
- ☐ Sewer Insulation

### ROOF

Y N
- ☐☐ Sagging Roof Line?
- ☐☐ Discoloration?
- ☐☐ Holes?

### FOUNDATION, DRIVEWAY, & POOL

**FOUNDATION**
- ☐ Visible Cracks? _____________

**DRIVEWAY**
- ☐ Visible Cracks? _____________

**POOL**
- ☐ Visible Cracks? _____________
- ☐ Above Ground? _____________

### GARAGE

Y N
- ☐☐ Functional - Manual?
- ☐☐ Functional - Remote?
- ☐ N/A

### SIDING

Y N
- ☐☐ Paint Peeling?
- ☐☐ Cracks/Splits?

### LANDSCAPING & CURB APPEAL

- ☐ Trees - Condition?
  _____________

- ☐ Lawn [*front*] - Condition?
  _____________

- ☐ Lawn [*back*] - Condition?
  _____________

- ☐ Fences - Condition?
  _____________

- ☐ Landscaping - Condition?
  _____________

8

# PROPERTY INFORMATION

| ADDRESS | |
|---|---|
| BEDROOMS | | BATHROOMS | | Sq. Ft. | |
| LOT SIZE | | YEAR BUILT | | SCHOOL DISTRICT | |
| ANNUAL TAX | | PRICE | |

# REALTOR INFORMATION

| NAME | |
|---|---|
| AGENCY | |
| PHONE | |
| EMAIL | |

## NOTES AND REMINDERS

# INSPECTION CHECKLIST

## INTERIOR

### FLOORING, WINDOWS & CEILING

**FLOOR**

☐ Age?

☐ Condition? _____________

**WINDOWS**

☐ Condition? _____________

**CEILING**

☐ Condition? _____________

### ROOMS

Y N

☐☐ Natural Lighting?

☐☐ Even Floors?

☐☐ Smoke Detectors?

☐☐ Carbon Monoxide Detector?

### WALLS

Y N

☐☐ Stains?

☐☐ Need Re-painting?

☐☐ Soundproof?

### STAIRS

Y N

☐☐ Creaky?

☐☐ Signs of Damage?

### DOORS

Y N

☐☐ Open & Close Property

☐☐ Weather Proofed

☐☐ Working Doorbell

### BATHROOM

Y N

☐☐ Stain-free?

☐☐ Mildew/Mold-free?

☐☐ Leak-free?

☐☐ Cabinet & Storage Space?

☐☐ Working Fans?

☐☐ Functioning Toilet?

### KITCHEN

Y N

☐☐ Stain-free?

☐☐ Mildew/Mold-free?

☐☐ Leak-free?

☐☐ Cabinet & Storage Space?

☐☐ Working Fans?

☐☐ Working Garbage Disposal?

## EXTERIOR

### UP-TO-DATE SYSTEMS

☐ Hire Home Inspector [*before purchase*]

☐ Electrical

☐ A/C

☐ Heating

☐ Security

☐ Plumbing

☐ Water

☐ Sewer Insulation

### ROOF

Y N

☐☐ Sagging Roof Line?

☐☐ Discoloration?

☐☐ Holes?

### FOUNDATION, DRIVEWAY, & POOL

**FOUNDATION**

☐ Visible Cracks? _____________

**DRIVEWAY**

☐ Visible Cracks? _____________

**POOL**

☐ Visible Cracks? _____________

☐ Above Ground? _____________

### GARAGE

Y N

☐☐ Functional - Manual?

☐☐ Functional - Remote?

☐ N/A

### SIDING

Y N

☐☐ Paint Peeling?

☐☐ Cracks/Splits?

### LANDSCAPING & CURB APPEAL

☐ Trees - Condition?

_____________

☐ Lawn [*front*] - Condition?

_____________

☐ Lawn [*back*] - Condition?

_____________

☐ Fences - Condition?

_____________

☐ Landscaping - Condition?

_____________

# 9

# PROPERTY INFORMATION

| ADDRESS | |
|---|---|
| BEDROOMS | | BATHROOMS | | Sq. Ft. | |
| LOT SIZE | | YEAR BUILT | | SCHOOL DISTRICT | |
| ANNUAL TAX | | PRICE | |

# REALTOR INFORMATION

| NAME | |
|---|---|
| AGENCY | |
| PHONE | |
| EMAIL | |

## NOTES AND REMINDERS

# INSPECTION CHECKLIST

## INTERIOR

### FLOORING, WINDOWS & CEILING

**FLOOR**

☐ Age?

☐ Condition? _____________

**WINDOWS**

☐ Condition? _____________

**CEILING**

☐ Condition? _____________

### ROOMS

Y N

☐☐ Natural Lighting?

☐☐ Even Floors?

☐☐ Smoke Detectors?

☐☐ Carbon Monoxide Detector?

### WALLS

Y N

☐☐ Stains?

☐☐ Need Re-painting?

☐☐ Soundproof?

### STAIRS

Y N

☐☐ Creaky?

☐☐ Signs of Damage?

### DOORS

Y N

☐☐ Open & Close Property

☐☐ Weather Proofed

☐☐ Working Doorbell

### BATHROOM

Y N

☐☐ Stain-free?

☐☐ Mildew/Mold-free?

☐☐ Leak-free?

☐☐ Cabinet & Storage Space?

☐☐ Working Fans?

☐☐ Functioning Toilet?

### KITCHEN

Y N

☐☐ Stain-free?

☐☐ Mildew/Mold-free?

☐☐ Leak-free?

☐☐ Cabinet & Storage Space?

☐☐ Working Fans?

☐☐ Working Garbage Disposal?

## EXTERIOR

### UP-TO-DATE SYSTEMS

☐ Hire Home Inspector [*before purchase*]

☐ Electrical

☐ A/C

☐ Heating

☐ Security

☐ Plumbing

☐ Water

☐ Sewer Insulation

### ROOF

Y N

☐☐ Sagging Roof Line?

☐☐ Discoloration?

☐☐ Holes?

### FOUNDATION, DRIVEWAY, & POOL

**FOUNDATION**

☐ Visible Cracks? ___________

**DRIVEWAY**

☐ Visible Cracks? ___________

**POOL**

☐ Visible Cracks? ___________

☐ Above Ground? ___________

### GARAGE

Y N

☐☐ Functional - Manual?

☐☐ Functional - Remote?

☐ N/A

### SIDING

Y N

☐☐ Paint Peeling?

☐☐ Cracks/Splits?

### LANDSCAPING & CURB APPEAL

☐ Trees - Condition?

_______________________

☐ Lawn [*front*] - Condition?

_______________________

☐ Lawn [*back*] - Condition?

_______________________

☐ Fences - Condition?

_______________________

☐ Landscaping - Condition?

_______________________

# 10

# PROPERTY INFORMATION

| ADDRESS | | | | | | |
|---|---|---|---|---|---|---|
| BEDROOMS | | BATHROOMS | | Sq. Ft. | | |
| LOT SIZE | | YEAR BUILT | | SCHOOL DISTRICT | | |
| ANNUAL TAX | | PRICE | | | | |

# REALTOR INFORMATION

| NAME | |
|---|---|
| AGENCY | |
| PHONE | |
| EMAIL | |

## NOTES AND REMINDERS

# INSPECTION CHECKLIST

## INTERIOR

### FLOORING, WINDOWS & CEILING

**FLOOR**
- ☐ Age?
- ☐ Condition? _____________

**WINDOWS**
- ☐ Condition? _____________

**CEILING**
- ☐ Condition? _____________

### ROOMS

Y N
- ☐☐ Natural Lighting?
- ☐☐ Even Floors?
- ☐☐ Smoke Detectors?
- ☐☐ Carbon Monoxide Detector?

### WALLS

Y N
- ☐☐ Stains?
- ☐☐ Need Re-painting?
- ☐☐ Soundproof?

### STAIRS

Y N
- ☐☐ Creaky?
- ☐☐ Signs of Damage?

### DOORS

Y N
- ☐☐ Open & Close Property
- ☐☐ Weather Proofed
- ☐☐ Working Doorbell

### BATHROOM

Y N
- ☐☐ Stain-free?
- ☐☐ Mildew/Mold-free?
- ☐☐ Leak-free?
- ☐☐ Cabinet & Storage Space?
- ☐☐ Working Fans?
- ☐☐ Functioning Toilet?

### KITCHEN

Y N
- ☐☐ Stain-free?
- ☐☐ Mildew/Mold-free?
- ☐☐ Leak-free?
- ☐☐ Cabinet & Storage Space?
- ☐☐ Working Fans?
- ☐☐ Working Garbage Disposal?

## EXTERIOR

### UP-TO-DATE SYSTEMS

- ☐ Hire Home Inspector [*before purchase*]
- ☐ Electrical
- ☐ A/C
- ☐ Heating
- ☐ Security
- ☐ Plumbing
- ☐ Water
- ☐ Sewer Insulation

### ROOF

Y N
- ☐☐ Sagging Roof Line?
- ☐☐ Discoloration?
- ☐☐ Holes?

### FOUNDATION, DRIVEWAY, & POOL

**FOUNDATION**
- ☐ Visible Cracks? ___________

**DRIVEWAY**
- ☐ Visible Cracks? ___________

**POOL**
- ☐ Visible Cracks? ___________
- ☐ Above Ground? ___________

### GARAGE

Y N
- ☐☐ Functional - Manual?
- ☐☐ Functional - Remote?
- ☐ N/A

### SIDING

Y N
- ☐☐ Paint Peeling?
- ☐☐ Cracks/Splits?

### LANDSCAPING & CURB APPEAL

- ☐ Trees - Condition?

_____________________________

- ☐ Lawn [*front*] - Condition?

_____________________________

- ☐ Lawn [*back*] - Condition?

_____________________________

- ☐ Fences - Condition?

_____________________________

- ☐ Landscaping - Condition?

_____________________________

# 11

# PROPERTY INFORMATION

| ADDRESS | |
|---|---|

| BEDROOMS | | BATHROOMS | | Sq. Ft. | |
|---|---|---|---|---|---|
| LOT SIZE | | YEAR BUILT | | SCHOOL DISTRICT | |
| ANNUAL TAX | | PRICE | | | |

# REALTOR INFORMATION

| NAME | |
|---|---|
| AGENCY | |
| PHONE | |
| EMAIL | |

## NOTES AND REMINDERS

# INSPECTION CHECKLIST

## INTERIOR

### FLOORING, WINDOWS & CEILING

**FLOOR**
- ☐ Age?
- ☐ Condition? ___________

**WINDOWS**
- ☐ Condition? ___________

**CEILING**
- ☐ Condition? ___________

### ROOMS

Y N
- ☐☐ Natural Lighting?
- ☐☐ Even Floors?
- ☐☐ Smoke Detectors?
- ☐☐ Carbon Monoxide Detector?

### WALLS

Y N
- ☐☐ Stains?
- ☐☐ Need Re-painting?
- ☐☐ Soundproof?

### STAIRS

Y N
- ☐☐ Creaky?
- ☐☐ Signs of Damage?

### DOORS

Y N
- ☐☐ Open & Close Property
- ☐☐ Weather Proofed
- ☐☐ Working Doorbell

### BATHROOM

Y N
- ☐☐ Stain-free?
- ☐☐ Mildew/Mold-free?
- ☐☐ Leak-free?
- ☐☐ Cabinet & Storage Space?
- ☐☐ Working Fans?
- ☐☐ Functioning Toilet?

### KITCHEN

Y N
- ☐☐ Stain-free?
- ☐☐ Mildew/Mold-free?
- ☐☐ Leak-free?
- ☐☐ Cabinet & Storage Space?
- ☐☐ Working Fans?
- ☐☐ Working Garbage Disposal?

## EXTERIOR

### UP-TO-DATE SYSTEMS

- ☐ Hire Home Inspector [*before purchase*]
- ☐ Electrical
- ☐ A/C
- ☐ Heating
- ☐ Security
- ☐ Plumbing
- ☐ Water
- ☐ Sewer Insulation

### ROOF

Y N
- ☐☐ Sagging Roof Line?
- ☐☐ Discoloration?
- ☐☐ Holes?

### FOUNDATION, DRIVEWAY, & POOL

**FOUNDATION**
- ☐ Visible Cracks? ___________

**DRIVEWAY**
- ☐ Visible Cracks? ___________

**POOL**
- ☐ Visible Cracks? ___________
- ☐ Above Ground? ___________

### GARAGE

Y N
- ☐☐ Functional - Manual?
- ☐☐ Functional - Remote?
- ☐ N/A

### SIDING

Y N
- ☐☐ Paint Peeling?
- ☐☐ Cracks/Splits?

### LANDSCAPING & CURB APPEAL

- ☐ Trees - Condition?

  ___________________________

- ☐ Lawn [*front*] - Condition?

  ___________________________

- ☐ Lawn [*back*] - Condition?

  ___________________________

- ☐ Fences - Condition?

  ___________________________

- ☐ Landscaping - Condition?

  ___________________________

# 12

# PROPERTY INFORMATION

| ADDRESS | |
|---|---|
| **BEDROOMS** | | **BATHROOMS** | | **Sq. Ft.** | |
| **LOT SIZE** | | **YEAR BUILT** | | **SCHOOL DISTRICT** | |
| **ANNUAL TAX** | | **PRICE** | |

# REALTOR INFORMATION

| NAME | |
|---|---|
| AGENCY | |
| PHONE | |
| EMAIL | |

## NOTES AND REMINDERS

# INSPECTION CHECKLIST

## INTERIOR

### FLOORING, WINDOWS & CEILING

**FLOOR**
- ☐ Age?
- ☐ Condition? _____________

**WINDOWS**
- ☐ Condition? _____________

**CEILING**
- ☐ Condition? _____________

### ROOMS

Y N
- ☐☐ Natural Lighting?
- ☐☐ Even Floors?
- ☐☐ Smoke Detectors?
- ☐☐ Carbon Monoxide Detector?

### WALLS

Y N
- ☐☐ Stains?
- ☐☐ Need Re-painting?
- ☐☐ Soundproof?

### STAIRS

Y N
- ☐☐ Creaky?
- ☐☐ Signs of Damage?

### DOORS

Y N
- ☐☐ Open & Close Property
- ☐☐ Weather Proofed
- ☐☐ Working Doorbell

### BATHROOM

Y N
- ☐☐ Stain-free?
- ☐☐ Mildew/Mold-free?
- ☐☐ Leak-free?
- ☐☐ Cabinet & Storage Space?
- ☐☐ Working Fans?
- ☐☐ Functioning Toilet?

### KITCHEN

Y N
- ☐☐ Stain-free?
- ☐☐ Mildew/Mold-free?
- ☐☐ Leak-free?
- ☐☐ Cabinet & Storage Space?
- ☐☐ Working Fans?
- ☐☐ Working Garbage Disposal?

## EXTERIOR

### UP-TO-DATE SYSTEMS

- ☐ Hire Home Inspector [*before purchase*]
- ☐ Electrical
- ☐ A/C
- ☐ Heating
- ☐ Security
- ☐ Plumbing
- ☐ Water
- ☐ Sewer Insulation

### ROOF

Y N
- ☐☐ Sagging Roof Line?
- ☐☐ Discoloration?
- ☐☐ Holes?

### FOUNDATION, DRIVEWAY, & POOL

**FOUNDATION**
- ☐ Visible Cracks? _____________

**DRIVEWAY**
- ☐ Visible Cracks? _____________

**POOL**
- ☐ Visible Cracks? _____________
- ☐ Above Ground? _____________

### GARAGE

Y N
- ☐☐ Functional - Manual?
- ☐☐ Functional - Remote?
- ☐ N/A

### SIDING

Y N
- ☐☐ Paint Peeling?
- ☐☐ Cracks/Splits?

### LANDSCAPING & CURB APPEAL

- ☐ Trees - Condition?
  _____________
- ☐ Lawn [*front*] - Condition?
  _____________
- ☐ Lawn [*back*] - Condition?
  _____________
- ☐ Fences - Condition?
  _____________
- ☐ Landscaping - Condition?
  _____________

# 13

# PROPERTY INFORMATION

| ADDRESS | |
|---|---|
| BEDROOMS | | BATHROOMS | | Sq. Ft. | |
| LOT SIZE | | YEAR BUILT | | SCHOOL DISTRICT | |
| ANNUAL TAX | | PRICE | |

# REALTOR INFORMATION

| NAME | |
|---|---|
| AGENCY | |
| PHONE | |
| EMAIL | |

## NOTES AND REMINDERS

# INSPECTION CHECKLIST

## INTERIOR

### FLOORING, WINDOWS & CEILING

**FLOOR**

- ☐ Age?
- ☐ Condition? _____________

**WINDOWS**

- ☐ Condition? _____________

**CEILING**

- ☐ Condition? _____________

### ROOMS

Y N

- ☐☐ Natural Lighting?
- ☐☐ Even Floors?
- ☐☐ Smoke Detectors?
- ☐☐ Carbon Monoxide Detector?

### WALLS

Y N

- ☐☐ Stains?
- ☐☐ Need Re-painting?
- ☐☐ Soundproof?

### STAIRS

Y N

- ☐☐ Creaky?
- ☐☐ Signs of Damage?

### DOORS

Y N

- ☐☐ Open & Close Property
- ☐☐ Weather Proofed
- ☐☐ Working Doorbell

### BATHROOM

Y N

- ☐☐ Stain-free?
- ☐☐ Mildew/Mold-free?
- ☐☐ Leak-free?
- ☐☐ Cabinet & Storage Space?
- ☐☐ Working Fans?
- ☐☐ Functioning Toilet?

### KITCHEN

Y N

- ☐☐ Stain-free?
- ☐☐ Mildew/Mold-free?
- ☐☐ Leak-free?
- ☐☐ Cabinet & Storage Space?
- ☐☐ Working Fans?
- ☐☐ Working Garbage Disposal?

## EXTERIOR

### UP-TO-DATE SYSTEMS

- ☐ Hire Home Inspector [*before purchase*]
- ☐ Electrical
- ☐ A/C
- ☐ Heating
- ☐ Security
- ☐ Plumbing
- ☐ Water
- ☐ Sewer Insulation

### ROOF

Y N

- ☐☐ Sagging Roof Line?
- ☐☐ Discoloration?
- ☐☐ Holes?

### FOUNDATION, DRIVEWAY, & POOL

**FOUNDATION**

- ☐ Visible Cracks? _____________

**DRIVEWAY**

- ☐ Visible Cracks? _____________

**POOL**

- ☐ Visible Cracks? _____________
- ☐ Above Ground? _____________

### GARAGE

Y N

- ☐☐ Functional - Manual?
- ☐☐ Functional - Remote?
- ☐ N/A

### SIDING

Y N

- ☐☐ Paint Peeling?
- ☐☐ Cracks/Splits?

### LANDSCAPING & CURB APPEAL

- ☐ Trees - Condition?

  _____________

- ☐ Lawn [*front*] - Condition?

  _____________

- ☐ Lawn [*back*] - Condition?

  _____________

- ☐ Fences - Condition?

  _____________

- ☐ Landscaping - Condition?

  _____________

# 14

# PROPERTY INFORMATION

| ADDRESS | | | | | |
|---|---|---|---|---|---|
| BEDROOMS | | BATHROOMS | | Sq. Ft. | |
| LOT SIZE | | YEAR BUILT | | SCHOOL DISTRICT | |
| ANNUAL TAX | | PRICE | | | |

# REALTOR INFORMATION

| NAME | |
|---|---|
| AGENCY | |
| PHONE | |
| EMAIL | |

## NOTES AND REMINDERS

# INSPECTION CHECKLIST

## INTERIOR

### FLOORING, WINDOWS & CEILING

**FLOOR**

☐ Age?

☐ Condition? _____________

**WINDOWS**

☐ Condition? _____________

**CEILING**

☐ Condition? _____________

### ROOMS

Y N

☐☐ Natural Lighting?

☐☐ Even Floors?

☐☐ Smoke Detectors?

☐☐ Carbon Monoxide Detector?

### WALLS

Y N

☐☐ Stains?

☐☐ Need Re-painting?

☐☐ Soundproof?

### STAIRS

Y N

☐☐ Creaky?

☐☐ Signs of Damage?

### DOORS

Y N

☐☐ Open & Close Property

☐☐ Weather Proofed

☐☐ Working Doorbell

### BATHROOM

Y N

☐☐ Stain-free?

☐☐ Mildew/Mold-free?

☐☐ Leak-free?

☐☐ Cabinet & Storage Space?

☐☐ Working Fans?

☐☐ Functioning Toilet?

### KITCHEN

Y N

☐☐ Stain-free?

☐☐ Mildew/Mold-free?

☐☐ Leak-free?

☐☐ Cabinet & Storage Space?

☐☐ Working Fans?

☐☐ Working Garbage Disposal?

## EXTERIOR

### UP-TO-DATE SYSTEMS

☐ Hire Home Inspector [*before purchase*]

☐ Electrical

☐ A/C

☐ Heating

☐ Security

☐ Plumbing

☐ Water

☐ Sewer Insulation

### ROOF

Y N

☐☐ Sagging Roof Line?

☐☐ Discoloration?

☐☐ Holes?

### FOUNDATION, DRIVEWAY, & POOL

**FOUNDATION**

☐ Visible Cracks? _____________

**DRIVEWAY**

☐ Visible Cracks? _____________

**POOL**

☐ Visible Cracks? _____________

☐ Above Ground? _____________

### GARAGE

Y N

☐☐ Functional - Manual?

☐☐ Functional - Remote?

☐ N/A

### SIDING

Y N

☐☐ Paint Peeling?

☐☐ Cracks/Splits?

### LANDSCAPING & CURB APPEAL

☐ Trees - Condition?

_____________

☐ Lawn [*front*] - Condition?

_____________

☐ Lawn [*back*] - Condition?

_____________

☐ Fences - Condition?

_____________

☐ Landscaping - Condition?

_____________

15

# PROPERTY INFORMATION

| | | | | | | |
|---|---|---|---|---|---|---|
| **ADDRESS** | | | | | | |
| **BEDROOMS** | | **BATHROOMS** | | **Sq. Ft.** | | |
| **LOT SIZE** | | **YEAR BUILT** | | **SCHOOL DISTRICT** | | |
| **ANNUAL TAX** | | | **PRICE** | | | |

# REALTOR INFORMATION

| | |
|---|---|
| **NAME** | |
| **AGENCY** | |
| **PHONE** | |
| **EMAIL** | |

## NOTES AND REMINDERS

# INSPECTION CHECKLIST

## INTERIOR

### FLOORING, WINDOWS & CEILING

**FLOOR**
- ☐ Age?
- ☐ Condition? _______________

**WINDOWS**
- ☐ Condition? _______________

**CEILING**
- ☐ Condition? _______________

### ROOMS

Y N
- ☐☐ Natural Lighting?
- ☐☐ Even Floors?
- ☐☐ Smoke Detectors?
- ☐☐ Carbon Monoxide Detector?

### WALLS

Y N
- ☐☐ Stains?
- ☐☐ Need Re-painting?
- ☐☐ Soundproof?

### STAIRS

Y N
- ☐☐ Creaky?
- ☐☐ Signs of Damage?

### DOORS

Y N
- ☐☐ Open & Close Property
- ☐☐ Weather Proofed
- ☐☐ Working Doorbell

### BATHROOM

Y N
- ☐☐ Stain-free?
- ☐☐ Mildew/Mold-free?
- ☐☐ Leak-free?
- ☐☐ Cabinet & Storage Space?
- ☐☐ Working Fans?
- ☐☐ Functioning Toilet?

### KITCHEN

Y N
- ☐☐ Stain-free?
- ☐☐ Mildew/Mold-free?
- ☐☐ Leak-free?
- ☐☐ Cabinet & Storage Space?
- ☐☐ Working Fans?
- ☐☐ Working Garbage Disposal?

## EXTERIOR

### UP-TO-DATE SYSTEMS

- ☐ Hire Home Inspector [*before purchase*]
- ☐ Electrical
- ☐ A/C
- ☐ Heating
- ☐ Security
- ☐ Plumbing
- ☐ Water
- ☐ Sewer Insulation

### ROOF

Y N
- ☐☐ Sagging Roof Line?
- ☐☐ Discoloration?
- ☐☐ Holes?

### FOUNDATION, DRIVEWAY, & POOL

**FOUNDATION**
- ☐ Visible Cracks? ___________

**DRIVEWAY**
- ☐ Visible Cracks? ___________

**POOL**
- ☐ Visible Cracks? ___________
- ☐ Above Ground? ___________

### GARAGE

Y N
- ☐☐ Functional - Manual?
- ☐☐ Functional - Remote?
- ☐ N/A

### SIDING

Y N
- ☐☐ Paint Peeling?
- ☐☐ Cracks/Splits?

### LANDSCAPING & CURB APPEAL

- ☐ Trees - Condition?

  _______________

- ☐ Lawn [*front*] - Condition?

  _______________

- ☐ Lawn [*back*] - Condition?

  _______________

- ☐ Fences - Condition?

  _______________

- ☐ Landscaping - Condition?

  _______________

# 16

# PROPERTY INFORMATION

| ADDRESS | | | | |
|---|---|---|---|---|
| BEDROOMS | | BATHROOMS | | Sq. Ft. |
| LOT SIZE | | YEAR BUILT | | SCHOOL DISTRICT |
| ANNUAL TAX | | PRICE | | |

# REALTOR INFORMATION

| NAME | |
|---|---|
| AGENCY | |
| PHONE | |
| EMAIL | |

## NOTES AND REMINDERS

# INSPECTION CHECKLIST

## INTERIOR

### FLOORING, WINDOWS & CEILING

**FLOOR**
- ☐ Age?
- ☐ Condition? _______________

**WINDOWS**
- ☐ Condition? _______________

**CEILING**
- ☐ Condition? _______________

### ROOMS

Y N
- ☐☐ Natural Lighting?
- ☐☐ Even Floors?
- ☐☐ Smoke Detectors?
- ☐☐ Carbon Monoxide Detector?

### WALLS

Y N
- ☐☐ Stains?
- ☐☐ Need Re-painting?
- ☐☐ Soundproof?

### STAIRS

Y N
- ☐☐ Creaky?
- ☐☐ Signs of Damage?

### DOORS

Y N
- ☐☐ Open & Close Property
- ☐☐ Weather Proofed
- ☐☐ Working Doorbell

### BATHROOM

Y N
- ☐☐ Stain-free?
- ☐☐ Mildew/Mold-free?
- ☐☐ Leak-free?
- ☐☐ Cabinet & Storage Space?
- ☐☐ Working Fans?
- ☐☐ Functioning Toilet?

### KITCHEN

Y N
- ☐☐ Stain-free?
- ☐☐ Mildew/Mold-free?
- ☐☐ Leak-free?
- ☐☐ Cabinet & Storage Space?
- ☐☐ Working Fans?
- ☐☐ Working Garbage Disposal?

## EXTERIOR

### UP-TO-DATE SYSTEMS

- ☐ Hire Home Inspector [*before purchase*]
- ☐ Electrical
- ☐ A/C
- ☐ Heating
- ☐ Security
- ☐ Plumbing
- ☐ Water
- ☐ Sewer Insulation

### ROOF

Y N
- ☐☐ Sagging Roof Line?
- ☐☐ Discoloration?
- ☐☐ Holes?

### FOUNDATION, DRIVEWAY, & POOL

**FOUNDATION**
- ☐ Visible Cracks? ___________

**DRIVEWAY**
- ☐ Visible Cracks? ___________

**POOL**
- ☐ Visible Cracks? ___________
- ☐ Above Ground? ___________

### GARAGE

Y N
- ☐☐ Functional - Manual?
- ☐☐ Functional - Remote?
- ☐ N/A

### SIDING

Y N
- ☐☐ Paint Peeling?
- ☐☐ Cracks/Splits?

### LANDSCAPING & CURB APPEAL

- ☐ Trees - Condition?

_______________

- ☐ Lawn [*front*] - Condition?

_______________

- ☐ Lawn [*back*] - Condition?

_______________

- ☐ Fences - Condition?

_______________

- ☐ Landscaping - Condition?

_______________

17

# PROPERTY INFORMATION

| ADDRESS | |
|---|---|
| BEDROOMS | | BATHROOMS | | Sq. Ft. | |
| LOT SIZE | | YEAR BUILT | | SCHOOL DISTRICT | |
| ANNUAL TAX | | PRICE | |

# REALTOR INFORMATION

| NAME | |
|---|---|
| AGENCY | |
| PHONE | |
| EMAIL | |

## NOTES AND REMINDERS

# INSPECTION CHECKLIST

## INTERIOR

### FLOORING, WINDOWS & CEILING

**FLOOR**
- ☐ Age?
- ☐ Condition? _____________

**WINDOWS**
- ☐ Condition? _____________

**CEILING**
- ☐ Condition? _____________

### ROOMS

Y N
- ☐☐ Natural Lighting?
- ☐☐ Even Floors?
- ☐☐ Smoke Detectors?
- ☐☐ Carbon Monoxide Detector?

### WALLS

Y N
- ☐☐ Stains?
- ☐☐ Need Re-painting?
- ☐☐ Soundproof?

### STAIRS

Y N
- ☐☐ Creaky?
- ☐☐ Signs of Damage?

### DOORS

Y N
- ☐☐ Open & Close Property
- ☐☐ Weather Proofed
- ☐☐ Working Doorbell

### BATHROOM

Y N
- ☐☐ Stain-free?
- ☐☐ Mildew/Mold-free?
- ☐☐ Leak-free?
- ☐☐ Cabinet & Storage Space?
- ☐☐ Working Fans?
- ☐☐ Functioning Toilet?

### KITCHEN

Y N
- ☐☐ Stain-free?
- ☐☐ Mildew/Mold-free?
- ☐☐ Leak-free?
- ☐☐ Cabinet & Storage Space?
- ☐☐ Working Fans?
- ☐☐ Working Garbage Disposal?

## EXTERIOR

### UP-TO-DATE SYSTEMS

- ☐ Hire Home Inspector [*before purchase*]
- ☐ Electrical
- ☐ A/C
- ☐ Heating
- ☐ Security
- ☐ Plumbing
- ☐ Water
- ☐ Sewer Insulation

### ROOF

Y N
- ☐☐ Sagging Roof Line?
- ☐☐ Discoloration?
- ☐☐ Holes?

### FOUNDATION, DRIVEWAY, & POOL

**FOUNDATION**
- ☐ Visible Cracks? _________

**DRIVEWAY**
- ☐ Visible Cracks? _________

**POOL**
- ☐ Visible Cracks? _________
- ☐ Above Ground? _________

### GARAGE

Y N
- ☐☐ Functional - Manual?
- ☐☐ Functional - Remote?
- ☐ N/A

### SIDING

Y N
- ☐☐ Paint Peeling?
- ☐☐ Cracks/Splits?

### LANDSCAPING & CURB APPEAL

- ☐ Trees - Condition?

_____________________

- ☐ Lawn [*front*] - Condition?

_____________________

- ☐ Lawn [*back*] - Condition?

_____________________

- ☐ Fences - Condition?

_____________________

- ☐ Landscaping - Condition?

_____________________

# 18

# PROPERTY INFORMATION

| ADDRESS | |
|---|---|
| BEDROOMS | | BATHROOMS | | Sq. Ft. | |
| LOT SIZE | | YEAR BUILT | | SCHOOL DISTRICT | |
| ANNUAL TAX | | PRICE | |

# REALTOR INFORMATION

| NAME | |
|---|---|
| AGENCY | |
| PHONE | |
| EMAIL | |

## NOTES AND REMINDERS

# INSPECTION CHECKLIST

## INTERIOR

### FLOORING, WINDOWS & CEILING

**FLOOR**

☐ Age?

☐ Condition? ___________

**WINDOWS**

☐ Condition? ___________

**CEILING**

☐ Condition? ___________

### ROOMS

Y N

☐☐ Natural Lighting?

☐☐ Even Floors?

☐☐ Smoke Detectors?

☐☐ Carbon Monoxide Detector?

### WALLS

Y N

☐☐ Stains?

☐☐ Need Re-painting?

☐☐ Soundproof?

### STAIRS

Y N

☐☐ Creaky?

☐☐ Signs of Damage?

### DOORS

Y N

☐☐ Open & Close Property

☐☐ Weather Proofed

☐☐ Working Doorbell

### BATHROOM

Y N

☐☐ Stain-free?

☐☐ Mildew/Mold-free?

☐☐ Leak-free?

☐☐ Cabinet & Storage Space?

☐☐ Working Fans?

☐☐ Functioning Toilet?

### KITCHEN

Y N

☐☐ Stain-free?

☐☐ Mildew/Mold-free?

☐☐ Leak-free?

☐☐ Cabinet & Storage Space?

☐☐ Working Fans?

☐☐ Working Garbage Disposal?

## EXTERIOR

### UP-TO-DATE SYSTEMS

☐ Hire Home Inspector [*before purchase*]

☐ Electrical

☐ A/C

☐ Heating

☐ Security

☐ Plumbing

☐ Water

☐ Sewer Insulation

### ROOF

Y N

☐☐ Sagging Roof Line?

☐☐ Discoloration?

☐☐ Holes?

### FOUNDATION, DRIVEWAY, & POOL

**FOUNDATION**

☐ Visible Cracks? ___________

**DRIVEWAY**

☐ Visible Cracks? ___________

**POOL**

☐ Visible Cracks? ___________

☐ Above Ground? ___________

### GARAGE

Y N

☐☐ Functional - Manual?

☐☐ Functional - Remote?

☐ N/A

### SIDING

Y N

☐☐ Paint Peeling?

☐☐ Cracks/Splits?

### LANDSCAPING & CURB APPEAL

☐ Trees - Condition?

___________

☐ Lawn [*front*] - Condition?

___________

☐ Lawn [*back*] - Condition?

___________

☐ Fences - Condition?

___________

☐ Landscaping - Condition?

___________

19

# PROPERTY INFORMATION

| ADDRESS | | | | | |
|---|---|---|---|---|---|
| BEDROOMS | | BATHROOMS | | Sq. Ft. | |
| LOT SIZE | | YEAR BUILT | | SCHOOL DISTRICT | |
| ANNUAL TAX | | PRICE | | | |

# REALTOR INFORMATION

| NAME | |
|---|---|
| AGENCY | |
| PHONE | |
| EMAIL | |

## NOTES AND REMINDERS

# INSPECTION CHECKLIST

## INTERIOR

### FLOORING, WINDOWS & CEILING

**FLOOR**
- ☐ Age?
- ☐ Condition? _____________

**WINDOWS**
- ☐ Condition? _____________

**CEILING**
- ☐ Condition? _____________

### ROOMS

Y N
- ☐☐ Natural Lighting?
- ☐☐ Even Floors?
- ☐☐ Smoke Detectors?
- ☐☐ Carbon Monoxide Detector?

### WALLS

Y N
- ☐☐ Stains?
- ☐☐ Need Re-painting?
- ☐☐ Soundproof?

### STAIRS

Y N
- ☐☐ Creaky?
- ☐☐ Signs of Damage?

### DOORS

Y N
- ☐☐ Open & Close Property
- ☐☐ Weather Proofed
- ☐☐ Working Doorbell

### BATHROOM

Y N
- ☐☐ Stain-free?
- ☐☐ Mildew/Mold-free?
- ☐☐ Leak-free?
- ☐☐ Cabinet & Storage Space?
- ☐☐ Working Fans?
- ☐☐ Functioning Toilet?

### KITCHEN

Y N
- ☐☐ Stain-free?
- ☐☐ Mildew/Mold-free?
- ☐☐ Leak-free?
- ☐☐ Cabinet & Storage Space?
- ☐☐ Working Fans?
- ☐☐ Working Garbage Disposal?

## EXTERIOR

### UP-TO-DATE SYSTEMS

- ☐ Hire Home Inspector [*before purchase*]
- ☐ Electrical
- ☐ A/C
- ☐ Heating
- ☐ Security
- ☐ Plumbing
- ☐ Water
- ☐ Sewer Insulation

### ROOF

Y N
- ☐☐ Sagging Roof Line?
- ☐☐ Discoloration?
- ☐☐ Holes?

### FOUNDATION, DRIVEWAY, & POOL

**FOUNDATION**
- ☐ Visible Cracks? _____________

**DRIVEWAY**
- ☐ Visible Cracks? _____________

**POOL**
- ☐ Visible Cracks? _____________
- ☐ Above Ground? _____________

### GARAGE

Y N
- ☐☐ Functional - Manual?
- ☐☐ Functional - Remote?
- ☐ N/A

### SIDING

Y N
- ☐☐ Paint Peeling?
- ☐☐ Cracks/Splits?

### LANDSCAPING & CURB APPEAL

- ☐ Trees - Condition?

  _____________

- ☐ Lawn [*front*] - Condition?

  _____________

- ☐ Lawn [*back*] - Condition?

  _____________

- ☐ Fences - Condition?

  _____________

- ☐ Landscaping - Condition?

  _____________

## 20

# PROPERTY INFORMATION

| ADDRESS | |
|---|---|
| BEDROOMS | | BATHROOMS | | Sq. Ft. | |
| LOT SIZE | | YEAR BUILT | | SCHOOL DISTRICT | |
| ANNUAL TAX | | PRICE | |

# REALTOR INFORMATION

| NAME | |
|---|---|
| AGENCY | |
| PHONE | |
| EMAIL | |

## NOTES AND REMINDERS

# INSPECTION CHECKLIST

## INTERIOR

### FLOORING, WINDOWS & CEILING

**FLOOR**
- ☐ Age?
- ☐ Condition? _____________

**WINDOWS**
- ☐ Condition? _____________

**CEILING**
- ☐ Condition? _____________

### ROOMS

Y N
- ☐☐ Natural Lighting?
- ☐☐ Even Floors?
- ☐☐ Smoke Detectors?
- ☐☐ Carbon Monoxide Detector?

### WALLS

Y N
- ☐☐ Stains?
- ☐☐ Need Re-painting?
- ☐☐ Soundproof?

### STAIRS

Y N
- ☐☐ Creaky?
- ☐☐ Signs of Damage?

### DOORS

Y N
- ☐☐ Open & Close Property
- ☐☐ Weather Proofed
- ☐☐ Working Doorbell

### BATHROOM

Y N
- ☐☐ Stain-free?
- ☐☐ Mildew/Mold-free?
- ☐☐ Leak-free?
- ☐☐ Cabinet & Storage Space?
- ☐☐ Working Fans?
- ☐☐ Functioning Toilet?

### KITCHEN

Y N
- ☐☐ Stain-free?
- ☐☐ Mildew/Mold-free?
- ☐☐ Leak-free?
- ☐☐ Cabinet & Storage Space?
- ☐☐ Working Fans?
- ☐☐ Working Garbage Disposal?

## EXTERIOR

### UP-TO-DATE SYSTEMS

- ☐ Hire Home Inspector [*before purchase*]
- ☐ Electrical
- ☐ A/C
- ☐ Heating
- ☐ Security
- ☐ Plumbing
- ☐ Water
- ☐ Sewer Insulation

### ROOF

Y N
- ☐☐ Sagging Roof Line?
- ☐☐ Discoloration?
- ☐☐ Holes?

### FOUNDATION, DRIVEWAY, & POOL

**FOUNDATION**
- ☐ Visible Cracks? _____________

**DRIVEWAY**
- ☐ Visible Cracks? _____________

**POOL**
- ☐ Visible Cracks? _____________
- ☐ Above Ground? _____________

### GARAGE

Y N
- ☐☐ Functional - Manual?
- ☐☐ Functional - Remote?
- ☐ N/A

### SIDING

Y N
- ☐☐ Paint Peeling?
- ☐☐ Cracks/Splits?

### LANDSCAPING & CURB APPEAL

- ☐ Trees - Condition?
_____________

- ☐ Lawn [*front*] - Condition?
_____________

- ☐ Lawn [*back*] - Condition?
_____________

- ☐ Fences - Condition?
_____________

- ☐ Landscaping - Condition?
_____________

# 21

# PROPERTY INFORMATION

| ADDRESS | | | |
|---|---|---|---|
| BEDROOMS | | BATHROOMS | Sq. Ft. |
| LOT SIZE | | YEAR BUILT | SCHOOL DISTRICT |
| ANNUAL TAX | | PRICE | |

# REALTOR INFORMATION

| NAME | |
|---|---|
| AGENCY | |
| PHONE | |
| EMAIL | |

## NOTES AND REMINDERS

# INSPECTION CHECKLIST

## INTERIOR

### FLOORING, WINDOWS & CEILING

**FLOOR**

☐ Age?

☐ Condition? ____________

**WINDOWS**

☐ Condition? ____________

**CEILING**

☐ Condition? ____________

### ROOMS

Y N

☐☐ Natural Lighting?

☐☐ Even Floors?

☐☐ Smoke Detectors?

☐☐ Carbon Monoxide Detector?

### WALLS

Y N

☐☐ Stains?

☐☐ Need Re-painting?

☐☐ Soundproof?

### STAIRS

Y N

☐☐ Creaky?

☐☐ Signs of Damage?

### DOORS

Y N

☐☐ Open & Close Property

☐☐ Weather Proofed

☐☐ Working Doorbell

### BATHROOM

Y N

☐☐ Stain-free?

☐☐ Mildew/Mold-free?

☐☐ Leak-free?

☐☐ Cabinet & Storage Space?

☐☐ Working Fans?

☐☐ Functioning Toilet?

### KITCHEN

Y N

☐☐ Stain-free?

☐☐ Mildew/Mold-free?

☐☐ Leak-free?

☐☐ Cabinet & Storage Space?

☐☐ Working Fans?

☐☐ Working Garbage Disposal?

## EXTERIOR

### UP-TO-DATE SYSTEMS

☐ Hire Home Inspector [*before purchase*]

☐ Electrical

☐ A/C

☐ Heating

☐ Security

☐ Plumbing

☐ Water

☐ Sewer Insulation

### ROOF

Y N

☐☐ Sagging Roof Line?

☐☐ Discoloration?

☐☐ Holes?

### FOUNDATION, DRIVEWAY, & POOL

**FOUNDATION**

☐ Visible Cracks? __________

**DRIVEWAY**

☐ Visible Cracks? __________

**POOL**

☐ Visible Cracks? __________

☐ Above Ground? __________

### GARAGE

Y N

☐☐ Functional - Manual?

☐☐ Functional - Remote?

☐ N/A

### SIDING

Y N

☐☐ Paint Peeling?

☐☐ Cracks/Splits?

### LANDSCAPING & CURB APPEAL

☐ Trees - Condition?

____________________

☐ Lawn [*front*] - Condition?

____________________

☐ Lawn [*back*] - Condition?

____________________

☐ Fences - Condition?

____________________

☐ Landscaping - Condition?

____________________

22

# PROPERTY INFORMATION

| ADDRESS | |
| --- | --- |
| BEDROOMS | | BATHROOMS | | Sq. Ft. | |
| LOT SIZE | | YEAR BUILT | | SCHOOL DISTRICT | |
| ANNUAL TAX | | PRICE | |

# REALTOR INFORMATION

| NAME | |
| --- | --- |
| AGENCY | |
| PHONE | |
| EMAIL | |

## NOTES AND REMINDERS

# INSPECTION CHECKLIST

## INTERIOR

### FLOORING, WINDOWS & CEILING

**FLOOR**

☐ Age?

☐ Condition? ___________

**WINDOWS**

☐ Condition? ___________

**CEILING**

☐ Condition? ___________

### ROOMS

Y N

☐☐ Natural Lighting?

☐☐ Even Floors?

☐☐ Smoke Detectors?

☐☐ Carbon Monoxide Detector?

### WALLS

Y N

☐☐ Stains?

☐☐ Need Re-painting?

☐☐ Soundproof?

### STAIRS

Y N

☐☐ Creaky?

☐☐ Signs of Damage?

### DOORS

Y N

☐☐ Open & Close Property

☐☐ Weather Proofed

☐☐ Working Doorbell

### BATHROOM

Y N

☐☐ Stain-free?

☐☐ Mildew/Mold-free?

☐☐ Leak-free?

☐☐ Cabinet & Storage Space?

☐☐ Working Fans?

☐☐ Functioning Toilet?

### KITCHEN

Y N

☐☐ Stain-free?

☐☐ Mildew/Mold-free?

☐☐ Leak-free?

☐☐ Cabinet & Storage Space?

☐☐ Working Fans?

☐☐ Working Garbage Disposal?

## EXTERIOR

### UP-TO-DATE SYSTEMS

☐ Hire Home Inspector [*before purchase*]

☐ Electrical

☐ A/C

☐ Heating

☐ Security

☐ Plumbing

☐ Water

☐ Sewer Insulation

### ROOF

Y N

☐☐ Sagging Roof Line?

☐☐ Discoloration?

☐☐ Holes?

### FOUNDATION, DRIVEWAY, & POOL

**FOUNDATION**

☐ Visible Cracks? ___________

**DRIVEWAY**

☐ Visible Cracks? ___________

**POOL**

☐ Visible Cracks? ___________

☐ Above Ground? ___________

### GARAGE

Y N

☐☐ Functional - Manual?

☐☐ Functional - Remote?

☐ N/A

### SIDING

Y N

☐☐ Paint Peeling?

☐☐ Cracks/Splits?

### LANDSCAPING & CURB APPEAL

☐ Trees - Condition?

___________

☐ Lawn [*front*] - Condition?

___________

☐ Lawn [*back*] - Condition?

___________

☐ Fences - Condition?

___________

☐ Landscaping - Condition?

___________

# 23

# PROPERTY INFORMATION

| ADDRESS | |
|---|---|
| **BEDROOMS** | | **BATHROOMS** | | **Sq. Ft.** | |
| **LOT SIZE** | | **YEAR BUILT** | | **SCHOOL DISTRICT** | |
| **ANNUAL TAX** | | **PRICE** | |

# REALTOR INFORMATION

| NAME | |
|---|---|
| AGENCY | |
| PHONE | |
| EMAIL | |

## NOTES AND REMINDERS

# INSPECTION CHECKLIST

## INTERIOR

### FLOORING, WINDOWS & CEILING

**FLOOR**
- ☐ Age?
- ☐ Condition? _____________

**WINDOWS**
- ☐ Condition? _____________

**CEILING**
- ☐ Condition? _____________

### ROOMS

Y N
- ☐☐ Natural Lighting?
- ☐☐ Even Floors?
- ☐☐ Smoke Detectors?
- ☐☐ Carbon Monoxide Detector?

### WALLS

Y N
- ☐☐ Stains?
- ☐☐ Need Re-painting?
- ☐☐ Soundproof?

### STAIRS

Y N
- ☐☐ Creaky?
- ☐☐ Signs of Damage?

### DOORS

Y N
- ☐☐ Open & Close Property
- ☐☐ Weather Proofed
- ☐☐ Working Doorbell

### BATHROOM

Y N
- ☐☐ Stain-free?
- ☐☐ Mildew/Mold-free?
- ☐☐ Leak-free?
- ☐☐ Cabinet & Storage Space?
- ☐☐ Working Fans?
- ☐☐ Functioning Toilet?

### KITCHEN

Y N
- ☐☐ Stain-free?
- ☐☐ Mildew/Mold-free?
- ☐☐ Leak-free?
- ☐☐ Cabinet & Storage Space?
- ☐☐ Working Fans?
- ☐☐ Working Garbage Disposal?

## EXTERIOR

### UP-TO-DATE SYSTEMS

- ☐ Hire Home Inspector [*before purchase*]
- ☐ Electrical
- ☐ A/C
- ☐ Heating
- ☐ Security
- ☐ Plumbing
- ☐ Water
- ☐ Sewer Insulation

### ROOF

Y N
- ☐☐ Sagging Roof Line?
- ☐☐ Discoloration?
- ☐☐ Holes?

### FOUNDATION, DRIVEWAY, & POOL

**FOUNDATION**
- ☐ Visible Cracks? _____________

**DRIVEWAY**
- ☐ Visible Cracks? _____________

**POOL**
- ☐ Visible Cracks? _____________
- ☐ Above Ground? _____________

### GARAGE

Y N
- ☐☐ Functional - Manual?
- ☐☐ Functional - Remote?
- ☐ N/A

### SIDING

Y N
- ☐☐ Paint Peeling?
- ☐☐ Cracks/Splits?

### LANDSCAPING & CURB APPEAL

- ☐ Trees - Condition?

_____________

- ☐ Lawn [*front*] - Condition?

_____________

- ☐ Lawn [*back*] - Condition?

_____________

- ☐ Fences - Condition?

_____________

- ☐ Landscaping - Condition?

_____________

# 24

# PROPERTY INFORMATION

| ADDRESS | | | | | |
|---|---|---|---|---|---|
| BEDROOMS | | BATHROOMS | | Sq. Ft. | |
| LOT SIZE | | YEAR BUILT | | SCHOOL DISTRICT | |
| ANNUAL TAX | | PRICE | | | |

# REALTOR INFORMATION

| NAME | |
|---|---|
| AGENCY | |
| PHONE | |
| EMAIL | |

## NOTES AND REMINDERS

# INSPECTION CHECKLIST

## INTERIOR

### FLOORING, WINDOWS & CEILING

**FLOOR**

☐ Age?

☐ Condition? _____________

**WINDOWS**

☐ Condition? _____________

**CEILING**

☐ Condition? _____________

### ROOMS

Y N

☐☐ Natural Lighting?

☐☐ Even Floors?

☐☐ Smoke Detectors?

☐☐ Carbon Monoxide Detector?

### WALLS

Y N

☐☐ Stains?

☐☐ Need Re-painting?

☐☐ Soundproof?

### STAIRS

Y N

☐☐ Creaky?

☐☐ Signs of Damage?

### DOORS

Y N

☐☐ Open & Close Property

☐☐ Weather Proofed

☐☐ Working Doorbell

### BATHROOM

Y N

☐☐ Stain-free?

☐☐ Mildew/Mold-free?

☐☐ Leak-free?

☐☐ Cabinet & Storage Space?

☐☐ Working Fans?

☐☐ Functioning Toilet?

### KITCHEN

Y N

☐☐ Stain-free?

☐☐ Mildew/Mold-free?

☐☐ Leak-free?

☐☐ Cabinet & Storage Space?

☐☐ Working Fans?

☐☐ Working Garbage Disposal?

## EXTERIOR

### UP-TO-DATE SYSTEMS

☐ Hire Home Inspector [*before purchase*]

☐ Electrical

☐ A/C

☐ Heating

☐ Security

☐ Plumbing

☐ Water

☐ Sewer Insulation

### ROOF

Y N

☐☐ Sagging Roof Line?

☐☐ Discoloration?

☐☐ Holes?

### FOUNDATION, DRIVEWAY, & POOL

**FOUNDATION**

☐ Visible Cracks? _____________

**DRIVEWAY**

☐ Visible Cracks? _____________

**POOL**

☐ Visible Cracks? _____________

☐ Above Ground? _____________

### GARAGE

Y N

☐☐ Functional - Manual?

☐☐ Functional - Remote?

☐ N/A

### SIDING

Y N

☐☐ Paint Peeling?

☐☐ Cracks/Splits?

### LANDSCAPING & CURB APPEAL

☐ Trees - Condition?

_____________

☐ Lawn [*front*] - Condition?

_____________

☐ Lawn [*back*] - Condition?

_____________

☐ Fences - Condition?

_____________

☐ Landscaping - Condition?

_____________

# 25

# PROPERTY INFORMATION

| ADDRESS | |
|---|---|
| BEDROOMS | | BATHROOMS | | Sq. Ft. | |
| LOT SIZE | | YEAR BUILT | | SCHOOL DISTRICT | |
| ANNUAL TAX | | PRICE | |

# REALTOR INFORMATION

| NAME | |
|---|---|
| AGENCY | |
| PHONE | |
| EMAIL | |

## NOTES AND REMINDERS

# INSPECTION CHECKLIST

## INTERIOR

### FLOORING, WINDOWS & CEILING

**FLOOR**

☐ Age?

☐ Condition? ____________

**WINDOWS**

☐ Condition? ____________

**CEILING**

☐ Condition? ____________

### ROOMS

Y N

☐☐ Natural Lighting?

☐☐ Even Floors?

☐☐ Smoke Detectors?

☐☐ Carbon Monoxide Detector?

### WALLS

Y N

☐☐ Stains?

☐☐ Need Re-painting?

☐☐ Soundproof?

### STAIRS

Y N

☐☐ Creaky?

☐☐ Signs of Damage?

### DOORS

Y N

☐☐ Open & Close Property

☐☐ Weather Proofed

☐☐ Working Doorbell

### BATHROOM

Y N

☐☐ Stain-free?

☐☐ Mildew/Mold-free?

☐☐ Leak-free?

☐☐ Cabinet & Storage Space?

☐☐ Working Fans?

☐☐ Functioning Toilet?

### KITCHEN

Y N

☐☐ Stain-free?

☐☐ Mildew/Mold-free?

☐☐ Leak-free?

☐☐ Cabinet & Storage Space?

☐☐ Working Fans?

☐☐ Working Garbage Disposal?

## EXTERIOR

### UP-TO-DATE SYSTEMS

☐ Hire Home Inspector [*before purchase*]

☐ Electrical

☐ A/C

☐ Heating

☐ Security

☐ Plumbing

☐ Water

☐ Sewer Insulation

### ROOF

Y N

☐☐ Sagging Roof Line?

☐☐ Discoloration?

☐☐ Holes?

### FOUNDATION, DRIVEWAY, & POOL

**FOUNDATION**

☐ Visible Cracks? ____________

**DRIVEWAY**

☐ Visible Cracks? ____________

**POOL**

☐ Visible Cracks? ____________

☐ Above Ground? ____________

### GARAGE

Y N

☐☐ Functional - Manual?

☐☐ Functional - Remote?

☐ N/A

### SIDING

Y N

☐☐ Paint Peeling?

☐☐ Cracks/Splits?

### LANDSCAPING & CURB APPEAL

☐ Trees - Condition?

____________________

☐ Lawn [*front*] - Condition?

____________________

☐ Lawn [*back*] - Condition?

____________________

☐ Fences - Condition?

____________________

☐ Landscaping - Condition?

____________________

# 26

# PROPERTY INFORMATION

| ADDRESS | | | | | |
|---|---|---|---|---|---|
| BEDROOMS | | BATHROOMS | | Sq. Ft. | |
| LOT SIZE | | YEAR BUILT | | SCHOOL DISTRICT | |
| ANNUAL TAX | | PRICE | | | |

# REALTOR INFORMATION

| NAME | |
|---|---|
| AGENCY | |
| PHONE | |
| EMAIL | |

## NOTES AND REMINDERS

# INSPECTION CHECKLIST

## INTERIOR

### FLOORING, WINDOWS & CEILING

**FLOOR**

☐ Age?

☐ Condition? _______________

**WINDOWS**

☐ Condition? _______________

**CEILING**

☐ Condition? _______________

### ROOMS

Y N

☐☐ Natural Lighting?

☐☐ Even Floors?

☐☐ Smoke Detectors?

☐☐ Carbon Monoxide Detector?

### WALLS

Y N

☐☐ Stains?

☐☐ Need Re-painting?

☐☐ Soundproof?

### STAIRS

Y N

☐☐ Creaky?

☐☐ Signs of Damage?

### DOORS

Y N

☐☐ Open & Close Property

☐☐ Weather Proofed

☐☐ Working Doorbell

### BATHROOM

Y N

☐☐ Stain-free?

☐☐ Mildew/Mold-free?

☐☐ Leak-free?

☐☐ Cabinet & Storage Space?

☐☐ Working Fans?

☐☐ Functioning Toilet?

### KITCHEN

Y N

☐☐ Stain-free?

☐☐ Mildew/Mold-free?

☐☐ Leak-free?

☐☐ Cabinet & Storage Space?

☐☐ Working Fans?

☐☐ Working Garbage Disposal?

## EXTERIOR

### UP-TO-DATE SYSTEMS

☐ Hire Home Inspector [*before purchase*]

☐ Electrical

☐ A/C

☐ Heating

☐ Security

☐ Plumbing

☐ Water

☐ Sewer Insulation

### ROOF

Y N

☐☐ Sagging Roof Line?

☐☐ Discoloration?

☐☐ Holes?

### FOUNDATION, DRIVEWAY, & POOL

**FOUNDATION**

☐ Visible Cracks? ___________

**DRIVEWAY**

☐ Visible Cracks? ___________

**POOL**

☐ Visible Cracks? ___________

☐ Above Ground? ___________

### GARAGE

Y N

☐☐ Functional - Manual?

☐☐ Functional - Remote?

☐ N/A

### SIDING

Y N

☐☐ Paint Peeling?

☐☐ Cracks/Splits?

### LANDSCAPING & CURB APPEAL

☐ Trees - Condition?

_______________

☐ Lawn [*front*] - Condition?

_______________

☐ Lawn [*back*] - Condition?

_______________

☐ Fences - Condition?

_______________

☐ Landscaping - Condition?

_______________

# 27

# PROPERTY INFORMATION

| ADDRESS | | | | | |
|---|---|---|---|---|---|
| BEDROOMS | | BATHROOMS | | Sq. Ft. | |
| LOT SIZE | | YEAR BUILT | | SCHOOL DISTRICT | |
| ANNUAL TAX | | PRICE | | | |

# REALTOR INFORMATION

| NAME | |
|---|---|
| AGENCY | |
| PHONE | |
| EMAIL | |

## NOTES AND REMINDERS

# INSPECTION CHECKLIST

## INTERIOR

### FLOORING, WINDOWS & CEILING

**FLOOR**
- ☐ Age?
- ☐ Condition? ___________

**WINDOWS**
- ☐ Condition? ___________

**CEILING**
- ☐ Condition? ___________

### ROOMS

Y N
- ☐☐ Natural Lighting?
- ☐☐ Even Floors?
- ☐☐ Smoke Detectors?
- ☐☐ Carbon Monoxide Detector?

### WALLS

Y N
- ☐☐ Stains?
- ☐☐ Need Re-painting?
- ☐☐ Soundproof?

### STAIRS

Y N
- ☐☐ Creaky?
- ☐☐ Signs of Damage?

### DOORS

Y N
- ☐☐ Open & Close Property
- ☐☐ Weather Proofed
- ☐☐ Working Doorbell

### BATHROOM

Y N
- ☐☐ Stain-free?
- ☐☐ Mildew/Mold-free?
- ☐☐ Leak-free?
- ☐☐ Cabinet & Storage Space?
- ☐☐ Working Fans?
- ☐☐ Functioning Toilet?

### KITCHEN

Y N
- ☐☐ Stain-free?
- ☐☐ Mildew/Mold-free?
- ☐☐ Leak-free?
- ☐☐ Cabinet & Storage Space?
- ☐☐ Working Fans?
- ☐☐ Working Garbage Disposal?

## EXTERIOR

### UP-TO-DATE SYSTEMS

- ☐ Hire Home Inspector [*before purchase*]
- ☐ Electrical
- ☐ A/C
- ☐ Heating
- ☐ Security
- ☐ Plumbing
- ☐ Water
- ☐ Sewer Insulation

### ROOF

Y N
- ☐☐ Sagging Roof Line?
- ☐☐ Discoloration?
- ☐☐ Holes?

### FOUNDATION, DRIVEWAY, & POOL

**FOUNDATION**
- ☐ Visible Cracks? ___________

**DRIVEWAY**
- ☐ Visible Cracks? ___________

**POOL**
- ☐ Visible Cracks? ___________
- ☐ Above Ground? ___________

### GARAGE

Y N
- ☐☐ Functional - Manual?
- ☐☐ Functional - Remote?
- ☐ N/A

### SIDING

Y N
- ☐☐ Paint Peeling?
- ☐☐ Cracks/Splits?

### LANDSCAPING & CURB APPEAL

- ☐ Trees - Condition?
  ___________

- ☐ Lawn [*front*] - Condition?
  ___________

- ☐ Lawn [*back*] - Condition?
  ___________

- ☐ Fences - Condition?
  ___________

- ☐ Landscaping - Condition?
  ___________

# 28

# PROPERTY INFORMATION

| ADDRESS | | | | | |
|---|---|---|---|---|---|
| BEDROOMS | | BATHROOMS | | Sq. Ft. | |
| LOT SIZE | | YEAR BUILT | | SCHOOL DISTRICT | |
| ANNUAL TAX | | PRICE | | | |

# REALTOR INFORMATION

| NAME | |
|---|---|
| AGENCY | |
| PHONE | |
| EMAIL | |

## NOTES AND REMINDERS

# INSPECTION CHECKLIST

## INTERIOR

### FLOORING, WINDOWS & CEILING

**FLOOR**

☐ Age?

☐ Condition? _____________

**WINDOWS**

☐ Condition? _____________

**CEILING**

☐ Condition? _____________

### ROOMS

Y N

☐☐ Natural Lighting?

☐☐ Even Floors?

☐☐ Smoke Detectors?

☐☐ Carbon Monoxide Detector?

### WALLS

Y N

☐☐ Stains?

☐☐ Need Re-painting?

☐☐ Soundproof?

### STAIRS

Y N

☐☐ Creaky?

☐☐ Signs of Damage?

### DOORS

Y N

☐☐ Open & Close Property

☐☐ Weather Proofed

☐☐ Working Doorbell

### BATHROOM

Y N

☐☐ Stain-free?

☐☐ Mildew/Mold-free?

☐☐ Leak-free?

☐☐ Cabinet & Storage Space?

☐☐ Working Fans?

☐☐ Functioning Toilet?

### KITCHEN

Y N

☐☐ Stain-free?

☐☐ Mildew/Mold-free?

☐☐ Leak-free?

☐☐ Cabinet & Storage Space?

☐☐ Working Fans?

☐☐ Working Garbage Disposal?

## EXTERIOR

### UP-TO-DATE SYSTEMS

☐ Hire Home Inspector [*before purchase*]

☐ Electrical

☐ A/C

☐ Heating

☐ Security

☐ Plumbing

☐ Water

☐ Sewer Insulation

### ROOF

Y N

☐☐ Sagging Roof Line?

☐☐ Discoloration?

☐☐ Holes?

### FOUNDATION, DRIVEWAY, & POOL

**FOUNDATION**

☐ Visible Cracks? _____________

**DRIVEWAY**

☐ Visible Cracks? _____________

**POOL**

☐ Visible Cracks? _____________

☐ Above Ground? _____________

### GARAGE

Y N

☐☐ Functional - Manual?

☐☐ Functional - Remote?

☐ N/A

### SIDING

Y N

☐☐ Paint Peeling?

☐☐ Cracks/Splits?

### LANDSCAPING & CURB APPEAL

☐ Trees - Condition?

_____________

☐ Lawn [*front*] - Condition?

_____________

☐ Lawn [*back*] - Condition?

_____________

☐ Fences - Condition?

_____________

☐ Landscaping - Condition?

_____________

# 29

# PROPERTY INFORMATION

| ADDRESS | | | | | |
|---|---|---|---|---|---|
| BEDROOMS | | BATHROOMS | | Sq. Ft. | |
| LOT SIZE | | YEAR BUILT | | SCHOOL DISTRICT | |
| ANNUAL TAX | | PRICE | | | |

# REALTOR INFORMATION

| NAME | |
|---|---|
| AGENCY | |
| PHONE | |
| EMAIL | |

## NOTES AND REMINDERS

# INSPECTION CHECKLIST

## INTERIOR

### FLOORING, WINDOWS & CEILING

**FLOOR**

☐ Age?

☐ Condition? ____________

**WINDOWS**

☐ Condition? ____________

**CEILING**

☐ Condition? ____________

### ROOMS

Y N

☐☐ Natural Lighting?

☐☐ Even Floors?

☐☐ Smoke Detectors?

☐☐ Carbon Monoxide Detector?

### WALLS

Y N

☐☐ Stains?

☐☐ Need Re-painting?

☐☐ Soundproof?

### STAIRS

Y N

☐☐ Creaky?

☐☐ Signs of Damage?

### DOORS

Y N

☐☐ Open & Close Property

☐☐ Weather Proofed

☐☐ Working Doorbell

### BATHROOM

Y N

☐☐ Stain-free?

☐☐ Mildew/Mold-free?

☐☐ Leak-free?

☐☐ Cabinet & Storage Space?

☐☐ Working Fans?

☐☐ Functioning Toilet?

### KITCHEN

Y N

☐☐ Stain-free?

☐☐ Mildew/Mold-free?

☐☐ Leak-free?

☐☐ Cabinet & Storage Space?

☐☐ Working Fans?

☐☐ Working Garbage Disposal?

## EXTERIOR

### UP-TO-DATE SYSTEMS

☐ Hire Home Inspector [*before purchase*]

☐ Electrical

☐ A/C

☐ Heating

☐ Security

☐ Plumbing

☐ Water

☐ Sewer Insulation

### ROOF

Y N

☐☐ Sagging Roof Line?

☐☐ Discoloration?

☐☐ Holes?

### FOUNDATION, DRIVEWAY, & POOL

**FOUNDATION**

☐ Visible Cracks? __________

**DRIVEWAY**

☐ Visible Cracks? __________

**POOL**

☐ Visible Cracks? __________

☐ Above Ground? __________

### GARAGE

Y N

☐☐ Functional - Manual?

☐☐ Functional - Remote?

☐ N/A

### SIDING

Y N

☐☐ Paint Peeling?

☐☐ Cracks/Splits?

### LANDSCAPING & CURB APPEAL

☐ Trees - Condition?

____________________

☐ Lawn [*front*] - Condition?

____________________

☐ Lawn [*back*] - Condition?

____________________

☐ Fences - Condition?

____________________

☐ Landscaping - Condition?

____________________

**30**

# PROPERTY INFORMATION

| ADDRESS | |
|---|---|
| **BEDROOMS** | | **BATHROOMS** | | **Sq. Ft.** | |
| **LOT SIZE** | | **YEAR BUILT** | | **SCHOOL DISTRICT** | |
| **ANNUAL TAX** | | **PRICE** | |

# REALTOR INFORMATION

| NAME | |
|---|---|
| **AGENCY** | |
| **PHONE** | |
| **EMAIL** | |

## NOTES AND REMINDERS

# INSPECTION CHECKLIST

## INTERIOR

### FLOORING, WINDOWS & CEILING

**FLOOR**
- ☐ Age?
- ☐ Condition? _____________

**WINDOWS**
- ☐ Condition? _____________

**CEILING**
- ☐ Condition? _____________

### ROOMS

Y N
- ☐☐ Natural Lighting?
- ☐☐ Even Floors?
- ☐☐ Smoke Detectors?
- ☐☐ Carbon Monoxide Detector?

### WALLS

Y N
- ☐☐ Stains?
- ☐☐ Need Re-painting?
- ☐☐ Soundproof?

### STAIRS

Y N
- ☐☐ Creaky?
- ☐☐ Signs of Damage?

### DOORS

Y N
- ☐☐ Open & Close Property
- ☐☐ Weather Proofed
- ☐☐ Working Doorbell

### BATHROOM

Y N
- ☐☐ Stain-free?
- ☐☐ Mildew/Mold-free?
- ☐☐ Leak-free?
- ☐☐ Cabinet & Storage Space?
- ☐☐ Working Fans?
- ☐☐ Functioning Toilet?

### KITCHEN

Y N
- ☐☐ Stain-free?
- ☐☐ Mildew/Mold-free?
- ☐☐ Leak-free?
- ☐☐ Cabinet & Storage Space?
- ☐☐ Working Fans?
- ☐☐ Working Garbage Disposal?

## EXTERIOR

### UP-TO-DATE SYSTEMS

- ☐ Hire Home Inspector [*before purchase*]
- ☐ Electrical
- ☐ A/C
- ☐ Heating
- ☐ Security
- ☐ Plumbing
- ☐ Water
- ☐ Sewer Insulation

### ROOF

Y N
- ☐☐ Sagging Roof Line?
- ☐☐ Discoloration?
- ☐☐ Holes?

### FOUNDATION, DRIVEWAY, & POOL

**FOUNDATION**
- ☐ Visible Cracks? _____________

**DRIVEWAY**
- ☐ Visible Cracks? _____________

**POOL**
- ☐ Visible Cracks? _____________
- ☐ Above Ground? _____________

### GARAGE

Y N
- ☐☐ Functional - Manual?
- ☐☐ Functional - Remote?
- ☐ N/A

### SIDING

Y N
- ☐☐ Paint Peeling?
- ☐☐ Cracks/Splits?

### LANDSCAPING & CURB APPEAL

- ☐ Trees - Condition?

_____________________

- ☐ Lawn [*front*] - Condition?

_____________________

- ☐ Lawn [*back*] - Condition?

_____________________

- ☐ Fences - Condition?

_____________________

- ☐ Landscaping - Condition?

_____________________

# 31

# PROPERTY INFORMATION

| ADDRESS | | | | | |
|---|---|---|---|---|---|
| BEDROOMS | | BATHROOMS | | Sq. Ft. | |
| LOT SIZE | | YEAR BUILT | | SCHOOL DISTRICT | |
| ANNUAL TAX | | | PRICE | | |

# REALTOR INFORMATION

| NAME | |
|---|---|
| AGENCY | |
| PHONE | |
| EMAIL | |

## NOTES AND REMINDERS

# INSPECTION CHECKLIST

## INTERIOR

### FLOORING, WINDOWS & CEILING

**FLOOR**

☐ Age?

☐ Condition? _____________

**WINDOWS**

☐ Condition? _____________

**CEILING**

☐ Condition? _____________

### ROOMS

Y N

☐☐ Natural Lighting?

☐☐ Even Floors?

☐☐ Smoke Detectors?

☐☐ Carbon Monoxide Detector?

### WALLS

Y N

☐☐ Stains?

☐☐ Need Re-painting?

☐☐ Soundproof?

### STAIRS

Y N

☐☐ Creaky?

☐☐ Signs of Damage?

### DOORS

Y N

☐☐ Open & Close Property

☐☐ Weather Proofed

☐☐ Working Doorbell

### BATHROOM

Y N

☐☐ Stain-free?

☐☐ Mildew/Mold-free?

☐☐ Leak-free?

☐☐ Cabinet & Storage Space?

☐☐ Working Fans?

☐☐ Functioning Toilet?

### KITCHEN

Y N

☐☐ Stain-free?

☐☐ Mildew/Mold-free?

☐☐ Leak-free?

☐☐ Cabinet & Storage Space?

☐☐ Working Fans?

☐☐ Working Garbage Disposal?

## EXTERIOR

### UP-TO-DATE SYSTEMS

☐ Hire Home Inspector [*before purchase*]

☐ Electrical

☐ A/C

☐ Heating

☐ Security

☐ Plumbing

☐ Water

☐ Sewer Insulation

### ROOF

Y N

☐☐ Sagging Roof Line?

☐☐ Discoloration?

☐☐ Holes?

### FOUNDATION, DRIVEWAY, & POOL

**FOUNDATION**

☐ Visible Cracks? _____________

**DRIVEWAY**

☐ Visible Cracks? _____________

**POOL**

☐ Visible Cracks? _____________

☐ Above Ground? _____________

### GARAGE

Y N

☐☐ Functional - Manual?

☐☐ Functional - Remote?

☐ N/A

### SIDING

Y N

☐☐ Paint Peeling?

☐☐ Cracks/Splits?

### LANDSCAPING & CURB APPEAL

☐ Trees - Condition?

_____________

☐ Lawn [*front*] - Condition?

_____________

☐ Lawn [*back*] - Condition?

_____________

☐ Fences - Condition?

_____________

☐ Landscaping - Condition?

_____________

# 32

# PROPERTY INFORMATION

| ADDRESS | |
|---|---|
| BEDROOMS | | BATHROOMS | | Sq. Ft. | |
| LOT SIZE | | YEAR BUILT | | SCHOOL DISTRICT | |
| ANNUAL TAX | | PRICE | |

# REALTOR INFORMATION

| NAME | |
|---|---|
| AGENCY | |
| PHONE | |
| EMAIL | |

## NOTES AND REMINDERS

# INSPECTION CHECKLIST

## INTERIOR

### FLOORING, WINDOWS & CEILING

**FLOOR**
- [ ] Age?
- [ ] Condition? _____________

**WINDOWS**
- [ ] Condition? _____________

**CEILING**
- [ ] Condition? _____________

### ROOMS

Y N
- [ ] [ ] Natural Lighting?
- [ ] [ ] Even Floors?
- [ ] [ ] Smoke Detectors?
- [ ] [ ] Carbon Monoxide Detector?

### WALLS

Y N
- [ ] [ ] Stains?
- [ ] [ ] Need Re-painting?
- [ ] [ ] Soundproof?

### STAIRS

Y N
- [ ] [ ] Creaky?
- [ ] [ ] Signs of Damage?

### DOORS

Y N
- [ ] [ ] Open & Close Property
- [ ] [ ] Weather Proofed
- [ ] [ ] Working Doorbell

### BATHROOM

Y N
- [ ] [ ] Stain-free?
- [ ] [ ] Mildew/Mold-free?
- [ ] [ ] Leak-free?
- [ ] [ ] Cabinet & Storage Space?
- [ ] [ ] Working Fans?
- [ ] [ ] Functioning Toilet?

### KITCHEN

Y N
- [ ] [ ] Stain-free?
- [ ] [ ] Mildew/Mold-free?
- [ ] [ ] Leak-free?
- [ ] [ ] Cabinet & Storage Space?
- [ ] [ ] Working Fans?
- [ ] [ ] Working Garbage Disposal?

## EXTERIOR

### UP-TO-DATE SYSTEMS

- [ ] Hire Home Inspector [*before purchase*]
- [ ] Electrical
- [ ] A/C
- [ ] Heating
- [ ] Security
- [ ] Plumbing
- [ ] Water
- [ ] Sewer Insulation

### ROOF

Y N
- [ ] [ ] Sagging Roof Line?
- [ ] [ ] Discoloration?
- [ ] [ ] Holes?

### FOUNDATION, DRIVEWAY, & POOL

**FOUNDATION**
- [ ] Visible Cracks? ___________

**DRIVEWAY**
- [ ] Visible Cracks? ___________

**POOL**
- [ ] Visible Cracks? ___________
- [ ] Above Ground? ___________

### GARAGE

Y N
- [ ] [ ] Functional - Manual?
- [ ] [ ] Functional - Remote?
- [ ] N/A

### SIDING

Y N
- [ ] [ ] Paint Peeling?
- [ ] [ ] Cracks/Splits?

### LANDSCAPING & CURB APPEAL

- [ ] Trees - Condition?
  _______________________

- [ ] Lawn [*front*] - Condition?
  _______________________

- [ ] Lawn [*back*] - Condition?
  _______________________

- [ ] Fences - Condition?
  _______________________

- [ ] Landscaping - Condition?
  _______________________

# 33

# PROPERTY INFORMATION

| ADDRESS | |
| --- | --- |
| BEDROOMS | | BATHROOMS | | Sq. Ft. | |
| LOT SIZE | | YEAR BUILT | | SCHOOL DISTRICT | |
| ANNUAL TAX | | PRICE | |

# REALTOR INFORMATION

| NAME | |
| --- | --- |
| AGENCY | |
| PHONE | |
| EMAIL | |

## NOTES AND REMINDERS

# INSPECTION CHECKLIST

## INTERIOR

### FLOORING, WINDOWS & CEILING

**FLOOR**
- ☐ Age?
- ☐ Condition? ___________

**WINDOWS**
- ☐ Condition? ___________

**CEILING**
- ☐ Condition? ___________

### ROOMS

Y N
- ☐☐ Natural Lighting?
- ☐☐ Even Floors?
- ☐☐ Smoke Detectors?
- ☐☐ Carbon Monoxide Detector?

### WALLS

Y N
- ☐☐ Stains?
- ☐☐ Need Re-painting?
- ☐☐ Soundproof?

### STAIRS

Y N
- ☐☐ Creaky?
- ☐☐ Signs of Damage?

### DOORS

Y N
- ☐☐ Open & Close Property
- ☐☐ Weather Proofed
- ☐☐ Working Doorbell

### BATHROOM

Y N
- ☐☐ Stain-free?
- ☐☐ Mildew/Mold-free?
- ☐☐ Leak-free?
- ☐☐ Cabinet & Storage Space?
- ☐☐ Working Fans?
- ☐☐ Functioning Toilet?

### KITCHEN

Y N
- ☐☐ Stain-free?
- ☐☐ Mildew/Mold-free?
- ☐☐ Leak-free?
- ☐☐ Cabinet & Storage Space?
- ☐☐ Working Fans?
- ☐☐ Working Garbage Disposal?

## EXTERIOR

### UP-TO-DATE SYSTEMS

- ☐ Hire Home Inspector [*before purchase*]
- ☐ Electrical
- ☐ A/C
- ☐ Heating
- ☐ Security
- ☐ Plumbing
- ☐ Water
- ☐ Sewer Insulation

### ROOF

Y N
- ☐☐ Sagging Roof Line?
- ☐☐ Discoloration?
- ☐☐ Holes?

### FOUNDATION, DRIVEWAY, & POOL

**FOUNDATION**
- ☐ Visible Cracks? ___________

**DRIVEWAY**
- ☐ Visible Cracks? ___________

**POOL**
- ☐ Visible Cracks? ___________
- ☐ Above Ground? ___________

### GARAGE

Y N
- ☐☐ Functional - Manual?
- ☐☐ Functional - Remote?
- ☐ N/A

### SIDING

Y N
- ☐☐ Paint Peeling?
- ☐☐ Cracks/Splits?

### LANDSCAPING & CURB APPEAL

- ☐ Trees - Condition?
  ___________
- ☐ Lawn [*front*] - Condition?
  ___________
- ☐ Lawn [*back*] - Condition?
  ___________
- ☐ Fences - Condition?
  ___________
- ☐ Landscaping - Condition?
  ___________

# 34

# PROPERTY INFORMATION

| | | | | | |
|---|---|---|---|---|---|
| **ADDRESS** | | | | | |
| **BEDROOMS** | | **BATHROOMS** | | **Sq. Ft.** | |
| **LOT SIZE** | | **YEAR BUILT** | | **SCHOOL DISTRICT** | |
| **ANNUAL TAX** | | | **PRICE** | | |

# REALTOR INFORMATION

| | |
|---|---|
| **NAME** | |
| **AGENCY** | |
| **PHONE** | |
| **EMAIL** | |

## NOTES AND REMINDERS

# INSPECTION CHECKLIST

## INTERIOR

### FLOORING, WINDOWS & CEILING

**FLOOR**
- ☐ Age?
- ☐ Condition? ____________

**WINDOWS**
- ☐ Condition? ____________

**CEILING**
- ☐ Condition? ____________

### ROOMS

Y N
- ☐☐ Natural Lighting?
- ☐☐ Even Floors?
- ☐☐ Smoke Detectors?
- ☐☐ Carbon Monoxide Detector?

### WALLS

Y N
- ☐☐ Stains?
- ☐☐ Need Re-painting?
- ☐☐ Soundproof?

### STAIRS

Y N
- ☐☐ Creaky?
- ☐☐ Signs of Damage?

### DOORS

Y N
- ☐☐ Open & Close Property
- ☐☐ Weather Proofed
- ☐☐ Working Doorbell

### BATHROOM

Y N
- ☐☐ Stain-free?
- ☐☐ Mildew/Mold-free?
- ☐☐ Leak-free?
- ☐☐ Cabinet & Storage Space?
- ☐☐ Working Fans?
- ☐☐ Functioning Toilet?

### KITCHEN

Y N
- ☐☐ Stain-free?
- ☐☐ Mildew/Mold-free?
- ☐☐ Leak-free?
- ☐☐ Cabinet & Storage Space?
- ☐☐ Working Fans?
- ☐☐ Working Garbage Disposal?

## EXTERIOR

### UP-TO-DATE SYSTEMS

- ☐ Hire Home Inspector [*before purchase*]
- ☐ Electrical
- ☐ A/C
- ☐ Heating
- ☐ Security
- ☐ Plumbing
- ☐ Water
- ☐ Sewer Insulation

### ROOF

Y N
- ☐☐ Sagging Roof Line?
- ☐☐ Discoloration?
- ☐☐ Holes?

### FOUNDATION, DRIVEWAY, & POOL

**FOUNDATION**
- ☐ Visible Cracks? __________

**DRIVEWAY**
- ☐ Visible Cracks? __________

**POOL**
- ☐ Visible Cracks? __________
- ☐ Above Ground? __________

### GARAGE

Y N
- ☐☐ Functional - Manual?
- ☐☐ Functional - Remote?
- ☐ N/A

### SIDING

Y N
- ☐☐ Paint Peeling?
- ☐☐ Cracks/Splits?

### LANDSCAPING & CURB APPEAL

- ☐ Trees - Condition?

  ____________________________

- ☐ Lawn [*front*] - Condition?

  ____________________________

- ☐ Lawn [*back*] - Condition?

  ____________________________

- ☐ Fences - Condition?

  ____________________________

- ☐ Landscaping - Condition?

  ____________________________

## 35

# PROPERTY INFORMATION

| ADDRESS | |
|---|---|
| BEDROOMS | | BATHROOMS | | Sq. Ft. | |
| LOT SIZE | | YEAR BUILT | | SCHOOL DISTRICT | |
| ANNUAL TAX | | PRICE | |

# REALTOR INFORMATION

| NAME | |
|---|---|
| AGENCY | |
| PHONE | |
| EMAIL | |

## NOTES AND REMINDERS

# INSPECTION CHECKLIST

## INTERIOR

### FLOORING, WINDOWS & CEILING

**FLOOR**
- ☐ Age?
- ☐ Condition? _____________

**WINDOWS**
- ☐ Condition? _____________

**CEILING**
- ☐ Condition? _____________

### ROOMS

Y N
- ☐☐ Natural Lighting?
- ☐☐ Even Floors?
- ☐☐ Smoke Detectors?
- ☐☐ Carbon Monoxide Detector?

### WALLS

Y N
- ☐☐ Stains?
- ☐☐ Need Re-painting?
- ☐☐ Soundproof?

### STAIRS

Y N
- ☐☐ Creaky?
- ☐☐ Signs of Damage?

### DOORS

Y N
- ☐☐ Open & Close Property
- ☐☐ Weather Proofed
- ☐☐ Working Doorbell

### BATHROOM

Y N
- ☐☐ Stain-free?
- ☐☐ Mildew/Mold-free?
- ☐☐ Leak-free?
- ☐☐ Cabinet & Storage Space?
- ☐☐ Working Fans?
- ☐☐ Functioning Toilet?

### KITCHEN

Y N
- ☐☐ Stain-free?
- ☐☐ Mildew/Mold-free?
- ☐☐ Leak-free?
- ☐☐ Cabinet & Storage Space?
- ☐☐ Working Fans?
- ☐☐ Working Garbage Disposal?

## EXTERIOR

### UP-TO-DATE SYSTEMS

- ☐ Hire Home Inspector [*before purchase*]
- ☐ Electrical
- ☐ A/C
- ☐ Heating
- ☐ Security
- ☐ Plumbing
- ☐ Water
- ☐ Sewer Insulation

### ROOF

Y N
- ☐☐ Sagging Roof Line?
- ☐☐ Discoloration?
- ☐☐ Holes?

### FOUNDATION, DRIVEWAY, & POOL

**FOUNDATION**
- ☐ Visible Cracks? _____________

**DRIVEWAY**
- ☐ Visible Cracks? _____________

**POOL**
- ☐ Visible Cracks? _____________
- ☐ Above Ground? _____________

### GARAGE

Y N
- ☐☐ Functional - Manual?
- ☐☐ Functional - Remote?
- ☐ N/A

### SIDING

Y N
- ☐☐ Paint Peeling?
- ☐☐ Cracks/Splits?

### LANDSCAPING & CURB APPEAL

- ☐ Trees - Condition?

_____________

- ☐ Lawn [*front*] - Condition?

_____________

- ☐ Lawn [*back*] - Condition?

_____________

- ☐ Fences - Condition?

_____________

- ☐ Landscaping - Condition?

_____________

# 36

# PROPERTY INFORMATION

| ADDRESS | | | | | |
|---|---|---|---|---|---|
| BEDROOMS | | BATHROOMS | | Sq. Ft. | |
| LOT SIZE | | YEAR BUILT | | SCHOOL DISTRICT | |
| ANNUAL TAX | | PRICE | | | |

# REALTOR INFORMATION

| NAME | |
|---|---|
| AGENCY | |
| PHONE | |
| EMAIL | |

## NOTES AND REMINDERS

# INSPECTION CHECKLIST

## INTERIOR

### FLOORING, WINDOWS & CEILING

**FLOOR**
- ☐ Age?
- ☐ Condition? ______________

**WINDOWS**
- ☐ Condition? ______________

**CEILING**
- ☐ Condition? ______________

### ROOMS

Y N
- ☐☐ Natural Lighting?
- ☐☐ Even Floors?
- ☐☐ Smoke Detectors?
- ☐☐ Carbon Monoxide Detector?

### WALLS

Y N
- ☐☐ Stains?
- ☐☐ Need Re-painting?
- ☐☐ Soundproof?

### STAIRS

Y N
- ☐☐ Creaky?
- ☐☐ Signs of Damage?

### DOORS

Y N
- ☐☐ Open & Close Property
- ☐☐ Weather Proofed
- ☐☐ Working Doorbell

### BATHROOM

Y N
- ☐☐ Stain-free?
- ☐☐ Mildew/Mold-free?
- ☐☐ Leak-free?
- ☐☐ Cabinet & Storage Space?
- ☐☐ Working Fans?
- ☐☐ Functioning Toilet?

### KITCHEN

Y N
- ☐☐ Stain-free?
- ☐☐ Mildew/Mold-free?
- ☐☐ Leak-free?
- ☐☐ Cabinet & Storage Space?
- ☐☐ Working Fans?
- ☐☐ Working Garbage Disposal?

## EXTERIOR

### UP-TO-DATE SYSTEMS

- ☐ Hire Home Inspector [*before purchase*]
- ☐ Electrical
- ☐ A/C
- ☐ Heating
- ☐ Security
- ☐ Plumbing
- ☐ Water
- ☐ Sewer Insulation

### ROOF

Y N
- ☐☐ Sagging Roof Line?
- ☐☐ Discoloration?
- ☐☐ Holes?

### FOUNDATION, DRIVEWAY, & POOL

**FOUNDATION**
- ☐ Visible Cracks? ____________

**DRIVEWAY**
- ☐ Visible Cracks? ____________

**POOL**
- ☐ Visible Cracks? ____________
- ☐ Above Ground? ____________

### GARAGE

Y N
- ☐☐ Functional - Manual?
- ☐☐ Functional - Remote?
- ☐ N/A

### SIDING

Y N
- ☐☐ Paint Peeling?
- ☐☐ Cracks/Splits?

### LANDSCAPING & CURB APPEAL

- ☐ Trees - Condition?
  ____________________
- ☐ Lawn [*front*] - Condition?
  ____________________
- ☐ Lawn [*back*] - Condition?
  ____________________
- ☐ Fences - Condition?
  ____________________
- ☐ Landscaping - Condition?
  ____________________

# 37

# PROPERTY INFORMATION

| ADDRESS | | | | |
|---|---|---|---|---|
| BEDROOMS | | BATHROOMS | | Sq. Ft. |
| LOT SIZE | | YEAR BUILT | | SCHOOL DISTRICT |
| ANNUAL TAX | | PRICE | | |

# REALTOR INFORMATION

| NAME | |
|---|---|
| AGENCY | |
| PHONE | |
| EMAIL | |

## NOTES AND REMINDERS

# INSPECTION CHECKLIST

## INTERIOR

### FLOORING, WINDOWS & CEILING

**FLOOR**
- ☐ Age?
- ☐ Condition? _____________

**WINDOWS**
- ☐ Condition? _____________

**CEILING**
- ☐ Condition? _____________

### ROOMS

Y N
- ☐☐ Natural Lighting?
- ☐☐ Even Floors?
- ☐☐ Smoke Detectors?
- ☐☐ Carbon Monoxide Detector?

### WALLS

Y N
- ☐☐ Stains?
- ☐☐ Need Re-painting?
- ☐☐ Soundproof?

### STAIRS

Y N
- ☐☐ Creaky?
- ☐☐ Signs of Damage?

### DOORS

Y N
- ☐☐ Open & Close Property
- ☐☐ Weather Proofed
- ☐☐ Working Doorbell

### BATHROOM

Y N
- ☐☐ Stain-free?
- ☐☐ Mildew/Mold-free?
- ☐☐ Leak-free?
- ☐☐ Cabinet & Storage Space?
- ☐☐ Working Fans?
- ☐☐ Functioning Toilet?

### KITCHEN

Y N
- ☐☐ Stain-free?
- ☐☐ Mildew/Mold-free?
- ☐☐ Leak-free?
- ☐☐ Cabinet & Storage Space?
- ☐☐ Working Fans?
- ☐☐ Working Garbage Disposal?

## EXTERIOR

### UP-TO-DATE SYSTEMS

- ☐ Hire Home Inspector [*before purchase*]
- ☐ Electrical
- ☐ A/C
- ☐ Heating
- ☐ Security
- ☐ Plumbing
- ☐ Water
- ☐ Sewer Insulation

### ROOF

Y N
- ☐☐ Sagging Roof Line?
- ☐☐ Discoloration?
- ☐☐ Holes?

### FOUNDATION, DRIVEWAY, & POOL

**FOUNDATION**
- ☐ Visible Cracks? ___________

**DRIVEWAY**
- ☐ Visible Cracks? ___________

**POOL**
- ☐ Visible Cracks? ___________
- ☐ Above Ground? ___________

### GARAGE

Y N
- ☐☐ Functional - Manual?
- ☐☐ Functional - Remote?
- ☐ N/A

### SIDING

Y N
- ☐☐ Paint Peeling?
- ☐☐ Cracks/Splits?

### LANDSCAPING & CURB APPEAL

- ☐ Trees - Condition?

_____________________

- ☐ Lawn [*front*] - Condition?

_____________________

- ☐ Lawn [*back*] - Condition?

_____________________

- ☐ Fences - Condition?

_____________________

- ☐ Landscaping - Condition?

_____________________

# 38

# PROPERTY INFORMATION

| ADDRESS | | | | | |
|---|---|---|---|---|---|
| BEDROOMS | | BATHROOMS | | Sq. Ft. | |
| LOT SIZE | | YEAR BUILT | | SCHOOL DISTRICT | |
| ANNUAL TAX | | PRICE | | | |

# REALTOR INFORMATION

| NAME | |
|---|---|
| AGENCY | |
| PHONE | |
| EMAIL | |

## NOTES AND REMINDERS

# INSPECTION CHECKLIST

## INTERIOR

### FLOORING, WINDOWS & CEILING

**FLOOR**
- ☐ Age?
- ☐ Condition? _____________

**WINDOWS**
- ☐ Condition? _____________

**CEILING**
- ☐ Condition? _____________

### ROOMS

Y N
- ☐☐ Natural Lighting?
- ☐☐ Even Floors?
- ☐☐ Smoke Detectors?
- ☐☐ Carbon Monoxide Detector?

### WALLS

Y N
- ☐☐ Stains?
- ☐☐ Need Re-painting?
- ☐☐ Soundproof?

### STAIRS

Y N
- ☐☐ Creaky?
- ☐☐ Signs of Damage?

### DOORS

Y N
- ☐☐ Open & Close Property
- ☐☐ Weather Proofed
- ☐☐ Working Doorbell

### BATHROOM

Y N
- ☐☐ Stain-free?
- ☐☐ Mildew/Mold-free?
- ☐☐ Leak-free?
- ☐☐ Cabinet & Storage Space?
- ☐☐ Working Fans?
- ☐☐ Functioning Toilet?

### KITCHEN

Y N
- ☐☐ Stain-free?
- ☐☐ Mildew/Mold-free?
- ☐☐ Leak-free?
- ☐☐ Cabinet & Storage Space?
- ☐☐ Working Fans?
- ☐☐ Working Garbage Disposal?

## EXTERIOR

### UP-TO-DATE SYSTEMS

- ☐ Hire Home Inspector [*before purchase*]
- ☐ Electrical
- ☐ A/C
- ☐ Heating
- ☐ Security
- ☐ Plumbing
- ☐ Water
- ☐ Sewer Insulation

### ROOF

Y N
- ☐☐ Sagging Roof Line?
- ☐☐ Discoloration?
- ☐☐ Holes?

### FOUNDATION, DRIVEWAY, & POOL

**FOUNDATION**
- ☐ Visible Cracks? _________

**DRIVEWAY**
- ☐ Visible Cracks? _________

**POOL**
- ☐ Visible Cracks? _________
- ☐ Above Ground? _________

### GARAGE

Y N
- ☐☐ Functional - Manual?
- ☐☐ Functional - Remote?
- ☐ N/A

### SIDING

Y N
- ☐☐ Paint Peeling?
- ☐☐ Cracks/Splits?

### LANDSCAPING & CURB APPEAL

- ☐ Trees - Condition? _____________
- ☐ Lawn [*front*] - Condition? _____________
- ☐ Lawn [*back*] - Condition? _____________
- ☐ Fences - Condition? _____________
- ☐ Landscaping - Condition? _____________

# 39

# PROPERTY INFORMATION

| ADDRESS | | | | | |
|---|---|---|---|---|---|
| BEDROOMS | | BATHROOMS | | Sq. Ft. | |
| LOT SIZE | | YEAR BUILT | | SCHOOL DISTRICT | |
| ANNUAL TAX | | PRICE | | | |

# REALTOR INFORMATION

| NAME | |
|---|---|
| AGENCY | |
| PHONE | |
| EMAIL | |

## NOTES AND REMINDERS

# INSPECTION CHECKLIST

## INTERIOR

### FLOORING, WINDOWS & CEILING

**FLOOR**
- ☐ Age?
- ☐ Condition? ____________

**WINDOWS**
- ☐ Condition? ____________

**CEILING**
- ☐ Condition? ____________

### ROOMS

Y N
- ☐☐ Natural Lighting?
- ☐☐ Even Floors?
- ☐☐ Smoke Detectors?
- ☐☐ Carbon Monoxide Detector?

### WALLS

Y N
- ☐☐ Stains?
- ☐☐ Need Re-painting?
- ☐☐ Soundproof?

### STAIRS

Y N
- ☐☐ Creaky?
- ☐☐ Signs of Damage?

### DOORS

Y N
- ☐☐ Open & Close Property
- ☐☐ Weather Proofed
- ☐☐ Working Doorbell

### BATHROOM

Y N
- ☐☐ Stain-free?
- ☐☐ Mildew/Mold-free?
- ☐☐ Leak-free?
- ☐☐ Cabinet & Storage Space?
- ☐☐ Working Fans?
- ☐☐ Functioning Toilet?

### KITCHEN

Y N
- ☐☐ Stain-free?
- ☐☐ Mildew/Mold-free?
- ☐☐ Leak-free?
- ☐☐ Cabinet & Storage Space?
- ☐☐ Working Fans?
- ☐☐ Working Garbage Disposal?

## EXTERIOR

### UP-TO-DATE SYSTEMS

- ☐ Hire Home Inspector [*before purchase*]
- ☐ Electrical
- ☐ A/C
- ☐ Heating
- ☐ Security
- ☐ Plumbing
- ☐ Water
- ☐ Sewer Insulation

### ROOF

Y N
- ☐☐ Sagging Roof Line?
- ☐☐ Discoloration?
- ☐☐ Holes?

### FOUNDATION, DRIVEWAY, & POOL

**FOUNDATION**
- ☐ Visible Cracks? __________

**DRIVEWAY**
- ☐ Visible Cracks? __________

**POOL**
- ☐ Visible Cracks? __________
- ☐ Above Ground? __________

### GARAGE

Y N
- ☐☐ Functional - Manual?
- ☐☐ Functional - Remote?
- ☐ N/A

### SIDING

Y N
- ☐☐ Paint Peeling?
- ☐☐ Cracks/Splits?

### LANDSCAPING & CURB APPEAL

- ☐ Trees - Condition?

____________________

- ☐ Lawn [*front*] - Condition?

____________________

- ☐ Lawn [*back*] - Condition?

____________________

- ☐ Fences - Condition?

____________________

- ☐ Landscaping - Condition?

____________________

40

# PROPERTY INFORMATION

| ADDRESS | |
|---|---|
| BEDROOMS | | BATHROOMS | | Sq. Ft. | |
| LOT SIZE | | YEAR BUILT | | SCHOOL DISTRICT | |
| ANNUAL TAX | | PRICE | |

# REALTOR INFORMATION

| NAME | |
|---|---|
| AGENCY | |
| PHONE | |
| EMAIL | |

## NOTES AND REMINDERS

# INSPECTION CHECKLIST

## INTERIOR

### FLOORING, WINDOWS & CEILING

**FLOOR**
- ☐ Age?
- ☐ Condition? _____________

**WINDOWS**
- ☐ Condition? _____________

**CEILING**
- ☐ Condition? _____________

### ROOMS

Y N
- ☐☐ Natural Lighting?
- ☐☐ Even Floors?
- ☐☐ Smoke Detectors?
- ☐☐ Carbon Monoxide Detector?

### WALLS

Y N
- ☐☐ Stains?
- ☐☐ Need Re-painting?
- ☐☐ Soundproof?

### STAIRS

Y N
- ☐☐ Creaky?
- ☐☐ Signs of Damage?

### DOORS

Y N
- ☐☐ Open & Close Property
- ☐☐ Weather Proofed
- ☐☐ Working Doorbell

### BATHROOM

Y N
- ☐☐ Stain-free?
- ☐☐ Mildew/Mold-free?
- ☐☐ Leak-free?
- ☐☐ Cabinet & Storage Space?
- ☐☐ Working Fans?
- ☐☐ Functioning Toilet?

### KITCHEN

Y N
- ☐☐ Stain-free?
- ☐☐ Mildew/Mold-free?
- ☐☐ Leak-free?
- ☐☐ Cabinet & Storage Space?
- ☐☐ Working Fans?
- ☐☐ Working Garbage Disposal?

## EXTERIOR

### UP-TO-DATE SYSTEMS

- ☐ Hire Home Inspector [*before purchase*]
- ☐ Electrical
- ☐ A/C
- ☐ Heating
- ☐ Security
- ☐ Plumbing
- ☐ Water
- ☐ Sewer Insulation

### ROOF

Y N
- ☐☐ Sagging Roof Line?
- ☐☐ Discoloration?
- ☐☐ Holes?

### FOUNDATION, DRIVEWAY, & POOL

**FOUNDATION**
- ☐ Visible Cracks? ___________

**DRIVEWAY**
- ☐ Visible Cracks? ___________

**POOL**
- ☐ Visible Cracks? ___________
- ☐ Above Ground? ___________

### GARAGE

Y N
- ☐☐ Functional - Manual?
- ☐☐ Functional - Remote?
- ☐ N/A

### SIDING

Y N
- ☐☐ Paint Peeling?
- ☐☐ Cracks/Splits?

### LANDSCAPING & CURB APPEAL

- ☐ Trees - Condition?
  _____________________
- ☐ Lawn [*front*] - Condition?
  _____________________
- ☐ Lawn [*back*] - Condition?
  _____________________
- ☐ Fences - Condition?
  _____________________
- ☐ Landscaping - Condition?
  _____________________

# 41

# PROPERTY INFORMATION

| ADDRESS | | | | |
|---|---|---|---|---|
| BEDROOMS | | BATHROOMS | | Sq. Ft. |
| LOT SIZE | | YEAR BUILT | | SCHOOL DISTRICT |
| ANNUAL TAX | | PRICE | | |

# REALTOR INFORMATION

| NAME | |
|---|---|
| AGENCY | |
| PHONE | |
| EMAIL | |

## NOTES AND REMINDERS

# INSPECTION CHECKLIST

## INTERIOR

### FLOORING, WINDOWS & CEILING

**FLOOR**
- ☐ Age?
- ☐ Condition? ____________

**WINDOWS**
- ☐ Condition? ____________

**CEILING**
- ☐ Condition? ____________

### ROOMS

Y N
- ☐☐ Natural Lighting?
- ☐☐ Even Floors?
- ☐☐ Smoke Detectors?
- ☐☐ Carbon Monoxide Detector?

### WALLS

Y N
- ☐☐ Stains?
- ☐☐ Need Re-painting?
- ☐☐ Soundproof?

### STAIRS

Y N
- ☐☐ Creaky?
- ☐☐ Signs of Damage?

### DOORS

Y N
- ☐☐ Open & Close Property
- ☐☐ Weather Proofed
- ☐☐ Working Doorbell

### BATHROOM

Y N
- ☐☐ Stain-free?
- ☐☐ Mildew/Mold-free?
- ☐☐ Leak-free?
- ☐☐ Cabinet & Storage Space?
- ☐☐ Working Fans?
- ☐☐ Functioning Toilet?

### KITCHEN

Y N
- ☐☐ Stain-free?
- ☐☐ Mildew/Mold-free?
- ☐☐ Leak-free?
- ☐☐ Cabinet & Storage Space?
- ☐☐ Working Fans?
- ☐☐ Working Garbage Disposal?

## EXTERIOR

### UP-TO-DATE SYSTEMS

- ☐ Hire Home Inspector [*before purchase*]
- ☐ Electrical
- ☐ A/C
- ☐ Heating
- ☐ Security
- ☐ Plumbing
- ☐ Water
- ☐ Sewer Insulation

### ROOF

Y N
- ☐☐ Sagging Roof Line?
- ☐☐ Discoloration?
- ☐☐ Holes?

### FOUNDATION, DRIVEWAY, & POOL

**FOUNDATION**
- ☐ Visible Cracks? ____________

**DRIVEWAY**
- ☐ Visible Cracks? ____________

**POOL**
- ☐ Visible Cracks? ____________
- ☐ Above Ground? ____________

### GARAGE

Y N
- ☐☐ Functional - Manual?
- ☐☐ Functional - Remote?
- ☐ N/A

### SIDING

Y N
- ☐☐ Paint Peeling?
- ☐☐ Cracks/Splits?

### LANDSCAPING & CURB APPEAL

- ☐ Trees - Condition?
____________

- ☐ Lawn [*front*] - Condition?
____________

- ☐ Lawn [*back*] - Condition?
____________

- ☐ Fences - Condition?
____________

- ☐ Landscaping - Condition?
____________

42

# PROPERTY INFORMATION

| | | | | | |
|---|---|---|---|---|---|
| **ADDRESS** | | | | | |
| **BEDROOMS** | | **BATHROOMS** | | **Sq. Ft.** | |
| **LOT SIZE** | | **YEAR BUILT** | | **SCHOOL DISTRICT** | |
| **ANNUAL TAX** | | | **PRICE** | | |

# REALTOR INFORMATION

| | |
|---|---|
| **NAME** | |
| **AGENCY** | |
| **PHONE** | |
| **EMAIL** | |

## NOTES AND REMINDERS

# INSPECTION CHECKLIST

## INTERIOR

### FLOORING, WINDOWS & CEILING

**FLOOR**

- ☐ Age?
- ☐ Condition? _____________

**WINDOWS**

- ☐ Condition? _____________

**CEILING**

- ☐ Condition? _____________

### ROOMS

Y N

- ☐☐ Natural Lighting?
- ☐☐ Even Floors?
- ☐☐ Smoke Detectors?
- ☐☐ Carbon Monoxide Detector?

### WALLS

Y N

- ☐☐ Stains?
- ☐☐ Need Re-painting?
- ☐☐ Soundproof?

### STAIRS

Y N

- ☐☐ Creaky?
- ☐☐ Signs of Damage?

### DOORS

Y N

- ☐☐ Open & Close Property
- ☐☐ Weather Proofed
- ☐☐ Working Doorbell

### BATHROOM

Y N

- ☐☐ Stain-free?
- ☐☐ Mildew/Mold-free?
- ☐☐ Leak-free?
- ☐☐ Cabinet & Storage Space?
- ☐☐ Working Fans?
- ☐☐ Functioning Toilet?

### KITCHEN

Y N

- ☐☐ Stain-free?
- ☐☐ Mildew/Mold-free?
- ☐☐ Leak-free?
- ☐☐ Cabinet & Storage Space?
- ☐☐ Working Fans?
- ☐☐ Working Garbage Disposal?

## EXTERIOR

### UP-TO-DATE SYSTEMS

- ☐ Hire Home Inspector [*before purchase*]
- ☐ Electrical
- ☐ A/C
- ☐ Heating
- ☐ Security
- ☐ Plumbing
- ☐ Water
- ☐ Sewer Insulation

### ROOF

Y N

- ☐☐ Sagging Roof Line?
- ☐☐ Discoloration?
- ☐☐ Holes?

### FOUNDATION, DRIVEWAY, & POOL

**FOUNDATION**

- ☐ Visible Cracks? _____________

**DRIVEWAY**

- ☐ Visible Cracks? _____________

**POOL**

- ☐ Visible Cracks? _____________
- ☐ Above Ground? _____________

### GARAGE

Y N

- ☐☐ Functional - Manual?
- ☐☐ Functional - Remote?
- ☐ N/A

### SIDING

Y N

- ☐☐ Paint Peeling?
- ☐☐ Cracks/Splits?

### LANDSCAPING & CURB APPEAL

- ☐ Trees - Condition?

  _____________

- ☐ Lawn [*front*] - Condition?

  _____________

- ☐ Lawn [*back*] - Condition?

  _____________

- ☐ Fences - Condition?

  _____________

- ☐ Landscaping - Condition?

  _____________

## 43

# PROPERTY INFORMATION

| ADDRESS | |
|---|---|
| BEDROOMS | | BATHROOMS | | Sq. Ft. | |
| LOT SIZE | | YEAR BUILT | | SCHOOL DISTRICT | |
| ANNUAL TAX | | PRICE | |

# REALTOR INFORMATION

| NAME | |
|---|---|
| AGENCY | |
| PHONE | |
| EMAIL | |

## NOTES AND REMINDERS

# INSPECTION CHECKLIST

## INTERIOR

### FLOORING, WINDOWS & CEILING

**FLOOR**

☐ Age?

☐ Condition? _____________

**WINDOWS**

☐ Condition? _____________

**CEILING**

☐ Condition? _____________

### ROOMS

Y N

☐☐ Natural Lighting?

☐☐ Even Floors?

☐☐ Smoke Detectors?

☐☐ Carbon Monoxide Detector?

### WALLS

Y N

☐☐ Stains?

☐☐ Need Re-painting?

☐☐ Soundproof?

### STAIRS

Y N

☐☐ Creaky?

☐☐ Signs of Damage?

### DOORS

Y N

☐☐ Open & Close Property

☐☐ Weather Proofed

☐☐ Working Doorbell

### BATHROOM

Y N

☐☐ Stain-free?

☐☐ Mildew/Mold-free?

☐☐ Leak-free?

☐☐ Cabinet & Storage Space?

☐☐ Working Fans?

☐☐ Functioning Toilet?

### KITCHEN

Y N

☐☐ Stain-free?

☐☐ Mildew/Mold-free?

☐☐ Leak-free?

☐☐ Cabinet & Storage Space?

☐☐ Working Fans?

☐☐ Working Garbage Disposal?

## EXTERIOR

### UP-TO-DATE SYSTEMS

☐ Hire Home Inspector [*before purchase*]

☐ Electrical

☐ A/C

☐ Heating

☐ Security

☐ Plumbing

☐ Water

☐ Sewer Insulation

### ROOF

Y N

☐☐ Sagging Roof Line?

☐☐ Discoloration?

☐☐ Holes?

### FOUNDATION, DRIVEWAY, & POOL

**FOUNDATION**

☐ Visible Cracks? _____________

**DRIVEWAY**

☐ Visible Cracks? _____________

**POOL**

☐ Visible Cracks? _____________

☐ Above Ground? _____________

### GARAGE

Y N

☐☐ Functional - Manual?

☐☐ Functional - Remote?

☐ N/A

### SIDING

Y N

☐☐ Paint Peeling?

☐☐ Cracks/Splits?

### LANDSCAPING & CURB APPEAL

☐ Trees - Condition?

_____________

☐ Lawn [*front*] - Condition?

_____________

☐ Lawn [*back*] - Condition?

_____________

☐ Fences - Condition?

_____________

☐ Landscaping - Condition?

_____________

## 44

# PROPERTY INFORMATION

| ADDRESS | |
|---|---|
| BEDROOMS | | BATHROOMS | | Sq. Ft. | |
| LOT SIZE | | YEAR BUILT | | SCHOOL DISTRICT | |
| ANNUAL TAX | | PRICE | |

# REALTOR INFORMATION

| NAME | |
|---|---|
| AGENCY | |
| PHONE | |
| EMAIL | |

## NOTES AND REMINDERS

# INSPECTION CHECKLIST

## INTERIOR

### FLOORING, WINDOWS & CEILING

**FLOOR**

☐ Age?

☐ Condition? _____________

**WINDOWS**

☐ Condition? _____________

**CEILING**

☐ Condition? _____________

### ROOMS

Y N

☐☐ Natural Lighting?

☐☐ Even Floors?

☐☐ Smoke Detectors?

☐☐ Carbon Monoxide Detector?

### WALLS

Y N

☐☐ Stains?

☐☐ Need Re-painting?

☐☐ Soundproof?

### STAIRS

Y N

☐☐ Creaky?

☐☐ Signs of Damage?

### DOORS

Y N

☐☐ Open & Close Property

☐☐ Weather Proofed

☐☐ Working Doorbell

### BATHROOM

Y N

☐☐ Stain-free?

☐☐ Mildew/Mold-free?

☐☐ Leak-free?

☐☐ Cabinet & Storage Space?

☐☐ Working Fans?

☐☐ Functioning Toilet?

### KITCHEN

Y N

☐☐ Stain-free?

☐☐ Mildew/Mold-free?

☐☐ Leak-free?

☐☐ Cabinet & Storage Space?

☐☐ Working Fans?

☐☐ Working Garbage Disposal?

## EXTERIOR

### UP-TO-DATE SYSTEMS

☐ Hire Home Inspector [*before purchase*]

☐ Electrical

☐ A/C

☐ Heating

☐ Security

☐ Plumbing

☐ Water

☐ Sewer Insulation

### ROOF

Y N

☐☐ Sagging Roof Line?

☐☐ Discoloration?

☐☐ Holes?

### FOUNDATION, DRIVEWAY, & POOL

**FOUNDATION**

☐ Visible Cracks? _________

**DRIVEWAY**

☐ Visible Cracks? _________

**POOL**

☐ Visible Cracks? _________

☐ Above Ground? _________

### GARAGE

Y N

☐☐ Functional - Manual?

☐☐ Functional - Remote?

☐ N/A

### SIDING

Y N

☐☐ Paint Peeling?

☐☐ Cracks/Splits?

### LANDSCAPING & CURB APPEAL

☐ Trees - Condition?

_____________________

☐ Lawn [*front*] - Condition?

_____________________

☐ Lawn [*back*] - Condition?

_____________________

☐ Fences - Condition?

_____________________

☐ Landscaping - Condition?

_____________________

**45**

# PROPERTY INFORMATION

| ADDRESS | |
|---|---|
| **BEDROOMS** | | **BATHROOMS** | | **Sq. Ft.** | |
| **LOT SIZE** | | **YEAR BUILT** | | **SCHOOL DISTRICT** | |
| **ANNUAL TAX** | | **PRICE** | |

# REALTOR INFORMATION

| NAME | |
|---|---|
| AGENCY | |
| PHONE | |
| EMAIL | |

## NOTES AND REMINDERS

# INSPECTION CHECKLIST

## INTERIOR

### FLOORING, WINDOWS & CEILING

**FLOOR**

☐ Age?

☐ Condition? _____________

**WINDOWS**

☐ Condition? _____________

**CEILING**

☐ Condition? _____________

### ROOMS

Y N

☐☐ Natural Lighting?

☐☐ Even Floors?

☐☐ Smoke Detectors?

☐☐ Carbon Monoxide Detector?

### WALLS

Y N

☐☐ Stains?

☐☐ Need Re-painting?

☐☐ Soundproof?

### STAIRS

Y N

☐☐ Creaky?

☐☐ Signs of Damage?

### DOORS

Y N

☐☐ Open & Close Property

☐☐ Weather Proofed

☐☐ Working Doorbell

### BATHROOM

Y N

☐☐ Stain-free?

☐☐ Mildew/Mold-free?

☐☐ Leak-free?

☐☐ Cabinet & Storage Space?

☐☐ Working Fans?

☐☐ Functioning Toilet?

### KITCHEN

Y N

☐☐ Stain-free?

☐☐ Mildew/Mold-free?

☐☐ Leak-free?

☐☐ Cabinet & Storage Space?

☐☐ Working Fans?

☐☐ Working Garbage Disposal?

## EXTERIOR

### UP-TO-DATE SYSTEMS

☐ Hire Home Inspector [*before purchase*]

☐ Electrical

☐ A/C

☐ Heating

☐ Security

☐ Plumbing

☐ Water

☐ Sewer Insulation

### ROOF

Y N

☐☐ Sagging Roof Line?

☐☐ Discoloration?

☐☐ Holes?

### FOUNDATION, DRIVEWAY, & POOL

**FOUNDATION**

☐ Visible Cracks? _____________

**DRIVEWAY**

☐ Visible Cracks? _____________

**POOL**

☐ Visible Cracks? _____________

☐ Above Ground? _____________

### GARAGE

Y N

☐☐ Functional - Manual?

☐☐ Functional - Remote?

☐ N/A

### SIDING

Y N

☐☐ Paint Peeling?

☐☐ Cracks/Splits?

### LANDSCAPING & CURB APPEAL

☐ Trees - Condition?

_____________

☐ Lawn [*front*] - Condition?

_____________

☐ Lawn [*back*] - Condition?

_____________

☐ Fences - Condition?

_____________

☐ Landscaping - Condition?

_____________

46

# PROPERTY INFORMATION

| ADDRESS | | | | | |
|---|---|---|---|---|---|
| BEDROOMS | | BATHROOMS | | Sq. Ft. | |
| LOT SIZE | | YEAR BUILT | | SCHOOL DISTRICT | |
| ANNUAL TAX | | PRICE | | | |

# REALTOR INFORMATION

| NAME | |
|---|---|
| AGENCY | |
| PHONE | |
| EMAIL | |

## NOTES AND REMINDERS

# INSPECTION CHECKLIST

## INTERIOR

### FLOORING, WINDOWS & CEILING

**FLOOR**

☐ Age?

☐ Condition? ____________

**WINDOWS**

☐ Condition? ____________

**CEILING**

☐ Condition? ____________

### ROOMS

Y N

☐☐ Natural Lighting?

☐☐ Even Floors?

☐☐ Smoke Detectors?

☐☐ Carbon Monoxide Detector?

### WALLS

Y N

☐☐ Stains?

☐☐ Need Re-painting?

☐☐ Soundproof?

### STAIRS

Y N

☐☐ Creaky?

☐☐ Signs of Damage?

### DOORS

Y N

☐☐ Open & Close Property

☐☐ Weather Proofed

☐☐ Working Doorbell

### BATHROOM

Y N

☐☐ Stain-free?

☐☐ Mildew/Mold-free?

☐☐ Leak-free?

☐☐ Cabinet & Storage Space?

☐☐ Working Fans?

☐☐ Functioning Toilet?

### KITCHEN

Y N

☐☐ Stain-free?

☐☐ Mildew/Mold-free?

☐☐ Leak-free?

☐☐ Cabinet & Storage Space?

☐☐ Working Fans?

☐☐ Working Garbage Disposal?

## EXTERIOR

### UP-TO-DATE SYSTEMS

☐ Hire Home Inspector [*before purchase*]

☐ Electrical

☐ A/C

☐ Heating

☐ Security

☐ Plumbing

☐ Water

☐ Sewer Insulation

### ROOF

Y N

☐☐ Sagging Roof Line?

☐☐ Discoloration?

☐☐ Holes?

### FOUNDATION, DRIVEWAY, & POOL

**FOUNDATION**

☐ Visible Cracks? ____________

**DRIVEWAY**

☐ Visible Cracks? ____________

**POOL**

☐ Visible Cracks? ____________

☐ Above Ground? ____________

### GARAGE

Y N

☐☐ Functional - Manual?

☐☐ Functional - Remote?

☐ N/A

### SIDING

Y N

☐☐ Paint Peeling?

☐☐ Cracks/Splits?

### LANDSCAPING & CURB APPEAL

☐ Trees - Condition?

____________

☐ Lawn [*front*] - Condition?

____________

☐ Lawn [*back*] - Condition?

____________

☐ Fences - Condition?

____________

☐ Landscaping - Condition?

____________

# 47

# PROPERTY INFORMATION

| ADDRESS | |
|---|---|
| BEDROOMS | | BATHROOMS | | Sq. Ft. | |
| LOT SIZE | | YEAR BUILT | | SCHOOL DISTRICT | |
| ANNUAL TAX | | PRICE | |

# REALTOR INFORMATION

| NAME | |
|---|---|
| AGENCY | |
| PHONE | |
| EMAIL | |

## NOTES AND REMINDERS

# INSPECTION CHECKLIST

## INTERIOR

### FLOORING, WINDOWS & CEILING

**FLOOR**
- ☐ Age?
- ☐ Condition? _____________

**WINDOWS**
- ☐ Condition? _____________

**CEILING**
- ☐ Condition? _____________

### ROOMS

Y N
- ☐☐ Natural Lighting?
- ☐☐ Even Floors?
- ☐☐ Smoke Detectors?
- ☐☐ Carbon Monoxide Detector?

### WALLS

Y N
- ☐☐ Stains?
- ☐☐ Need Re-painting?
- ☐☐ Soundproof?

### STAIRS

Y N
- ☐☐ Creaky?
- ☐☐ Signs of Damage?

### DOORS

Y N
- ☐☐ Open & Close Property
- ☐☐ Weather Proofed
- ☐☐ Working Doorbell

### BATHROOM

Y N
- ☐☐ Stain-free?
- ☐☐ Mildew/Mold-free?
- ☐☐ Leak-free?
- ☐☐ Cabinet & Storage Space?
- ☐☐ Working Fans?
- ☐☐ Functioning Toilet?

### KITCHEN

Y N
- ☐☐ Stain-free?
- ☐☐ Mildew/Mold-free?
- ☐☐ Leak-free?
- ☐☐ Cabinet & Storage Space?
- ☐☐ Working Fans?
- ☐☐ Working Garbage Disposal?

## EXTERIOR

### UP-TO-DATE SYSTEMS

- ☐ Hire Home Inspector [*before purchase*]
- ☐ Electrical
- ☐ A/C
- ☐ Heating
- ☐ Security
- ☐ Plumbing
- ☐ Water
- ☐ Sewer Insulation

### ROOF

Y N
- ☐☐ Sagging Roof Line?
- ☐☐ Discoloration?
- ☐☐ Holes?

### FOUNDATION, DRIVEWAY, & POOL

**FOUNDATION**
- ☐ Visible Cracks? _____________

**DRIVEWAY**
- ☐ Visible Cracks? _____________

**POOL**
- ☐ Visible Cracks? _____________
- ☐ Above Ground? _____________

### GARAGE

Y N
- ☐☐ Functional - Manual?
- ☐☐ Functional - Remote?
- ☐ N/A

### SIDING

Y N
- ☐☐ Paint Peeling?
- ☐☐ Cracks/Splits?

### LANDSCAPING & CURB APPEAL

- ☐ Trees - Condition? _____________
- ☐ Lawn [*front*] - Condition? _____________
- ☐ Lawn [*back*] - Condition? _____________
- ☐ Fences - Condition? _____________
- ☐ Landscaping - Condition? _____________

48

# PROPERTY INFORMATION

| ADDRESS | |
|---|---|
| BEDROOMS | | BATHROOMS | | Sq. Ft. | |
| LOT SIZE | | YEAR BUILT | | SCHOOL DISTRICT | |
| ANNUAL TAX | | PRICE | |

# REALTOR INFORMATION

| NAME | |
|---|---|
| AGENCY | |
| PHONE | |
| EMAIL | |

## NOTES AND REMINDERS

# INSPECTION CHECKLIST

## INTERIOR

### FLOORING, WINDOWS & CEILING

**FLOOR**
- ☐ Age?
- ☐ Condition? _____________

**WINDOWS**
- ☐ Condition? _____________

**CEILING**
- ☐ Condition? _____________

### ROOMS

Y N
- ☐☐ Natural Lighting?
- ☐☐ Even Floors?
- ☐☐ Smoke Detectors?
- ☐☐ Carbon Monoxide Detector?

### WALLS

Y N
- ☐☐ Stains?
- ☐☐ Need Re-painting?
- ☐☐ Soundproof?

### STAIRS

Y N
- ☐☐ Creaky?
- ☐☐ Signs of Damage?

### DOORS

Y N
- ☐☐ Open & Close Property
- ☐☐ Weather Proofed
- ☐☐ Working Doorbell

### BATHROOM

Y N
- ☐☐ Stain-free?
- ☐☐ Mildew/Mold-free?
- ☐☐ Leak-free?
- ☐☐ Cabinet & Storage Space?
- ☐☐ Working Fans?
- ☐☐ Functioning Toilet?

### KITCHEN

Y N
- ☐☐ Stain-free?
- ☐☐ Mildew/Mold-free?
- ☐☐ Leak-free?
- ☐☐ Cabinet & Storage Space?
- ☐☐ Working Fans?
- ☐☐ Working Garbage Disposal?

## EXTERIOR

### UP-TO-DATE SYSTEMS

- ☐ Hire Home Inspector [*before purchase*]
- ☐ Electrical
- ☐ A/C
- ☐ Heating
- ☐ Security
- ☐ Plumbing
- ☐ Water
- ☐ Sewer Insulation

### ROOF

Y N
- ☐☐ Sagging Roof Line?
- ☐☐ Discoloration?
- ☐☐ Holes?

### FOUNDATION, DRIVEWAY, & POOL

**FOUNDATION**
- ☐ Visible Cracks? _____________

**DRIVEWAY**
- ☐ Visible Cracks? _____________

**POOL**
- ☐ Visible Cracks? _____________
- ☐ Above Ground? _____________

### GARAGE

Y N
- ☐☐ Functional - Manual?
- ☐☐ Functional - Remote?
- ☐ N/A

### SIDING

Y N
- ☐☐ Paint Peeling?
- ☐☐ Cracks/Splits?

### LANDSCAPING & CURB APPEAL

- ☐ Trees - Condition?

_____________

- ☐ Lawn [*front*] - Condition?

_____________

- ☐ Lawn [*back*] - Condition?

_____________

- ☐ Fences - Condition?

_____________

- ☐ Landscaping - Condition?

_____________

# 49

# PROPERTY INFORMATION

| ADDRESS | |
|---|---|
| BEDROOMS | | BATHROOMS | | Sq. Ft. | |
| LOT SIZE | | YEAR BUILT | | SCHOOL DISTRICT | |
| ANNUAL TAX | | PRICE | |

# REALTOR INFORMATION

| NAME | |
|---|---|
| AGENCY | |
| PHONE | |
| EMAIL | |

## NOTES AND REMINDERS

# INSPECTION CHECKLIST

## INTERIOR

### FLOORING, WINDOWS & CEILING

**FLOOR**

☐ Age?

☐ Condition? _____________

**WINDOWS**

☐ Condition? _____________

**CEILING**

☐ Condition? _____________

### ROOMS

Y N

☐☐ Natural Lighting?

☐☐ Even Floors?

☐☐ Smoke Detectors?

☐☐ Carbon Monoxide Detector?

### WALLS

Y N

☐☐ Stains?

☐☐ Need Re-painting?

☐☐ Soundproof?

### STAIRS

Y N

☐☐ Creaky?

☐☐ Signs of Damage?

### DOORS

Y N

☐☐ Open & Close Property

☐☐ Weather Proofed

☐☐ Working Doorbell

### BATHROOM

Y N

☐☐ Stain-free?

☐☐ Mildew/Mold-free?

☐☐ Leak-free?

☐☐ Cabinet & Storage Space?

☐☐ Working Fans?

☐☐ Functioning Toilet?

### KITCHEN

Y N

☐☐ Stain-free?

☐☐ Mildew/Mold-free?

☐☐ Leak-free?

☐☐ Cabinet & Storage Space?

☐☐ Working Fans?

☐☐ Working Garbage Disposal?

## EXTERIOR

### UP-TO-DATE SYSTEMS

☐ Hire Home Inspector [*before purchase*]

☐ Electrical

☐ A/C

☐ Heating

☐ Security

☐ Plumbing

☐ Water

☐ Sewer Insulation

### ROOF

Y N

☐☐ Sagging Roof Line?

☐☐ Discoloration?

☐☐ Holes?

### FOUNDATION, DRIVEWAY, & POOL

**FOUNDATION**

☐ Visible Cracks? _____________

**DRIVEWAY**

☐ Visible Cracks? _____________

**POOL**

☐ Visible Cracks? _____________

☐ Above Ground? _____________

### GARAGE

Y N

☐☐ Functional - Manual?

☐☐ Functional - Remote?

☐ N/A

### SIDING

Y N

☐☐ Paint Peeling?

☐☐ Cracks/Splits?

### LANDSCAPING & CURB APPEAL

☐ Trees - Condition?

_____________

☐ Lawn [*front*] - Condition?

_____________

☐ Lawn [*back*] - Condition?

_____________

☐ Fences - Condition?

_____________

☐ Landscaping - Condition?

_____________

50

# PROPERTY INFORMATION

| ADDRESS | | | | | |
|---|---|---|---|---|---|
| BEDROOMS | | BATHROOMS | | Sq. Ft. | |
| LOT SIZE | | YEAR BUILT | | SCHOOL DISTRICT | |
| ANNUAL TAX | | PRICE | | | |

# REALTOR INFORMATION

| NAME | |
|---|---|
| AGENCY | |
| PHONE | |
| EMAIL | |

## NOTES AND REMINDERS

# INSPECTION CHECKLIST

## INTERIOR

### FLOORING, WINDOWS & CEILING

**FLOOR**

☐ Age?

☐ Condition? _____________

**WINDOWS**

☐ Condition? _____________

**CEILING**

☐ Condition? _____________

### ROOMS

Y N

☐☐ Natural Lighting?

☐☐ Even Floors?

☐☐ Smoke Detectors?

☐☐ Carbon Monoxide Detector?

### WALLS

Y N

☐☐ Stains?

☐☐ Need Re-painting?

☐☐ Soundproof?

### STAIRS

Y N

☐☐ Creaky?

☐☐ Signs of Damage?

### DOORS

Y N

☐☐ Open & Close Property

☐☐ Weather Proofed

☐☐ Working Doorbell

### BATHROOM

Y N

☐☐ Stain-free?

☐☐ Mildew/Mold-free?

☐☐ Leak-free?

☐☐ Cabinet & Storage Space?

☐☐ Working Fans?

☐☐ Functioning Toilet?

### KITCHEN

Y N

☐☐ Stain-free?

☐☐ Mildew/Mold-free?

☐☐ Leak-free?

☐☐ Cabinet & Storage Space?

☐☐ Working Fans?

☐☐ Working Garbage Disposal?

## EXTERIOR

### UP-TO-DATE SYSTEMS

☐ Hire Home Inspector [*before purchase*]

☐ Electrical

☐ A/C

☐ Heating

☐ Security

☐ Plumbing

☐ Water

☐ Sewer Insulation

### ROOF

Y N

☐☐ Sagging Roof Line?

☐☐ Discoloration?

☐☐ Holes?

### FOUNDATION, DRIVEWAY, & POOL

**FOUNDATION**

☐ Visible Cracks? __________

**DRIVEWAY**

☐ Visible Cracks? __________

**POOL**

☐ Visible Cracks? __________

☐ Above Ground? __________

### GARAGE

Y N

☐☐ Functional - Manual?

☐☐ Functional - Remote?

☐ N/A

### SIDING

Y N

☐☐ Paint Peeling?

☐☐ Cracks/Splits?

### LANDSCAPING & CURB APPEAL

☐ Trees - Condition?

_____________________

☐ Lawn [*front*] - Condition?

_____________________

☐ Lawn [*back*] - Condition?

_____________________

☐ Fences - Condition?

_____________________

☐ Landscaping - Condition?

_____________________